G. T. HAWKER

Spell it yourself

Oxford University Press

Oxford University Press, Walton Street, Oxford, OX2 6DP

Oxford New York
Athens Auckland Bangkok Bogotá Bombay
Buenos Aires Calcutta Cape Town Dar es Salaam
Delhi Florence Hong Kong Istanbul Karachi
Kuala Lumpur Madras Madrid Melbourne
Mexico City Nairobi Paris Singapore
Taipei Tokyo Toronto

and associated companies in
Berlin Ibadan

Oxford is a trade mark of Oxford University Press

© G. T. Hawker 1981

First published in paperback 1962
Second edition in paperback 1981
Redesigned impression for paperback 1994

First published in hardback 1992
Redesigned impression for hardback 1995

paperback   10 9 8 7 6 5
hardback   10 9 8 7 6 5 4

ISBN 0 19 910342 9 (paperback)
ISBN 0 19 834138 5 (hardback)

A CIP catalogue record for this book is available from the British Library

Printed in Great Britain by The Bath Press, Bath

Contents

	Page
Instructions	iv
Word Lists	1
Boys' Names	108
Girls' Names	110
Numbers	112
Countries and Peoples of the World	114
Parts of Speech	116
Spelling Lists of Words to Learn	117
Contractions	130
Homophones	131
Multiplication Tables	133
Note for Teachers and Parents	134
Index	136

Instructions

1   Think hard about the word you wish to spell and try to decide with which two letters it starts.

2   Find these two letters in the Index and you will see the number of the page where the word can be found or where you should begin looking for it.

3   Turn to this page and look down the column under these two letters until you find the word you want. Where there are a lot of words which begin with the same two letters, the first three letters of the words are given at the top of the column to help you find the word you want.

It may be necessary to add the word endings shown in *italics* on the right-hand side of the column in order to build up the complete word you want, e.g.

rich   *er, est, ly, ness, es*
hair   *dresser, -dryer, pin, -slide, -style, s*

Here the words **richer, richest, richly, richness** and **riches** may be built up, and also **hairdresser(s), hair-dryer(s), hairpins(s), hair-slide(s), hair-style(s)** and **hairs.**

Where the last letter or letters of a word are in *italics* these must be left off before adding to the other endings, e.g.

happ*y*   *ier, iest, ily, iness.*

Here the *y* must be left off before making:

happier, happiest, happily, happiness.

The plurals of most nouns may be formed by adding the letter, or letters, shown in *italics* on the extreme right of the column. A few nouns have their plurals given in full on the right of the column, and you will notice that some nouns have two plurals, either of which may be used, e.g. **cactuses** or **cacti, hoofs** or **hooves, fish** or **fishes.**

All the words with *ed, ing* after them are verbs or may be used as verbs. If you require the word to end in either *ed* or *ing,* remember the following:

(a) **kick** *ed, ing, s* = **kicked   kicking   kicks**

Here *ed* or *ing* or *s* may be added to the verb without changing the word at all.

(b) **stab** *bed, bing, s* = **stabbed   stabbing   stabs**
   stop *ped, ping, s* = **stopped   stopping   stops**

Here you can see that the final consonant (the last letter) of these verbs has to be doubled before adding *ed* or *ing*.

(c) **blame** *d, ɇing, s* = **blamed   blaming   blames**

Where a verb ends in a letter **e** the *d* or *s* may be added to the word but the **e** must be dropped before adding *ing*. An *ɇ* is placed before the *ing* to remind you of this.

There are a few other verbs which change their endings in different ways. You will usually find these endings printed by the side of, above or below, the verb, e.g.

began   **lie** *d, s*   **carry** *ing*
begin *ning, s*   **lying**   **carr***ied* *ies*
begun

Warning: A word which has a star (*) after it has the same sound, or almost the same sound, as another word; but it has a different meaning and spelling, e.g. **knew* new*; their* there*; which* witch*.** The word endings will help you to decide which of these words you want and so will the words in brackets. These are included to guide you; they are not always exact definitions. The words are paired in small print at the bottom of the page. If you find that you have looked up the wrong word you may easily see how the other is spelt and where it may be found in its correct alphabetical place in the book.

ab   ac

ab		ac	
abandon	ed, ing, ment, s	academ y	ies
abate	d, ǿing, ment, s	accelerate	d, ǿing, s
abbess	es	accent	s
abbey	s	accept* (receive)	able, ed, ing, s
abbot	s	accident	al, ally, s
abduct	ed, ing, ion, s	accommodate	d, ǿing, s
abhor	red, ring, rence, rent, s	accommodation	
abide	d, ǿing, s	accompany	ing
abilit y	ies	accompan ied	ies
ablaze		accomplish	ed, ing, es
able	r, st, -bodied	according	ly
abnormal	ity, ly	account	ed, ing, ant, s
aboard		accumulate	d, ǿing, s
abolish	ed, ing, es	accuracy	
abominable		accurate	ly
abominate	d, ǿing, s	accusation	s
Aboriginal	s or Aborigines	accuse	d, ǿing, s
abound	ed, ing, s	accustom	ed, ing, s
about		ache	d, ǿing, s
above	-board	achieve	d, ǿing, ment, s
abreast		acid	s
abroad		acknowledge	d, ǿing, s
abrupt	ly, ness	acknowledg(e)ment	s
abscess	es	acorn	s
absence	s	acquaint	ed, ing, ance, s
absent	ed, ing, ly, ee, s	acquire	d, ǿing, ment, s
absent-minded	ly, ness	acre	age, s
absolute	ly	acrobat	ic, s
absorb	ed, ing, ent, s	across	
abstain	ed, ing, s	act	ed, ing, s
absurd	ity, ly	actor	s
abundance		actress	es
abundant	ly	action	s
abuse	d, ǿing, s	active	ly
abysmal	ly	activit y	ies
abyss	es	actual	ly

ǿ Drop **e** before adding *ing*

* accept
  except

ad ae af ag

ad	
adapt	able, ed, ing, or, s
add	ed, ing, s
addition	al, s
adder	s
address	ed, ing, es
adequate	ly
adhere	d, ∉ing, s
adhesive	s
adjective	s
adjoin	ed, ing, s
adjust	able, ed, ing, ment, s
admirabl e	y
admiral	s
admiration	
admire	d, ∉ing, r, s
admission	s
admit	ted, ting, s
admittance	
adopt	ed, ing, ion, s
adorabl e	y
adore	d, ∉ing, s
adorn	ed, ing, ment, s
adrift	
adult	s
advance	d, ∉ing, ment, s
advantage	s
adventure	d, ∉ing, r, s
adventurous	ly, ness
adverb	s
adversar y	ies
advertise	d, ∉ing, r, s
advertisement	s
advice	
advisable	
advise	d, ∉ing, r, s
advocate	d, ∉ing, s

ae	
aerial	s
aerodrome	s
aeronaut	ic, s
aeroplane	s

af	
affair	s
affect	ed, ing, s
affection	s
affectionate	ly, ness
affix	ed, ing, es
afford	ed, ing, s
afloat	
afraid	
after	
afternoon	s
afterwards	

ag	
again	
against	
age	d, less, -group, s
ageing or **aging**	
agent	s
aggravate	d, ∉ing, s
aggressive	ly, ness
aghast	
agile	ly
agilit y	ies
agitate	d, ∉ing, s
ago	
agonize	d, ∉ing, s
agon y	ies
agree	able, d, ing, ment, s
agricultur e	al
aground	

∉ Drop **e** before adding *ing*

ai

aid	ed, ing, s
ail* (be ill)	ed, ing, ment, s
aim	ed, ing, less, lessly, s
air*	ed, ing, crew, mail, tight, man, men
air*	gun, field, line, port, way, s
aircraft	-carrier
Airedale	s
air force	s
air y	ier, iest, ily, iness
aisle* (part of a church; gangway)	s

al

alarm	ed, ing, ist, -bell, -clock, s
album	s
alcohol	ism, ic, s
alcove	s
ale* (beer)	s
alert	ed, ing, ly, ness, s
algebra	
alibi	s
alien	s
alight	ed, ing, s
alike	
alive	
all right	
alley	way, s
alligator	s
allot	ted, ting, ment, s
allow	*ed, ing, ance, s
all y	ies
almond	-blossom, -paste, -tree, s
almost	
alone	
along	side
aloud* (loudly)	

alphabet	ical, ically, s
already	
Alsatian	s
also	
altar* (church table)	s
alter* (change)	ed, ing, ation, s
alternate	d, ∉ing, ly, s
alternative	ly, s
although	
altitude	s
altogether	
aluminium	
always	

am

amateur	ish, s
amaze	d, ∉ing, ment, s
amber	
ambition	s
ambitious	ly, ness
amble	d, ∉ing, s
ambulance	man, men, s
ambush	ed, ing, es
amend	ed, ing, ment, s
amiabl e	y
amid or **amidst**	
amiss	
ammunition	
among or **amongst**	
amount	ed, ing, s
amphibian	s or **amphibia**
amphibious	ly
ample	r, st, ness
amplifier	s
amputate	d, ∉ing, s
amuse	d, ∉ing, ment, s

∉ Drop **e** before adding *ing*

4

an

ap

an	
anaesthetic	*s*
ancestor	*s*
ancestr*y*	*ies*
anchor	*ed, ing, age, s*
ancient	*ly, ness, s*
anemone	*s*
angel	*s*
anger	*ed, ing, s*
angr*y*	*ier, iest, ily*
angle	*d, ȩing, r, s*
anguish	*ed, ing, es*
animal	*s*
ankle	*s*
anniversar*y*	*ies*
announce	*d, ȩing, r, ment, s*
annoy	*ed, ing, ance, s*
annual	*ly, s*
anoint	*ed, ing, ment, s*
anonymous	*ly*
anorak	*s*
another	
answer	*ed, ing, s*
ant	*-eater, -hill, s*
antarctic	
antelope	*s*
antic	*s*
anticipate	*d, ȩing, s*
anticipation	*s*
antique	*-dealer, -shop, s*
antirrhinum	*s*
antiseptic	*s*
antler	*s*
anvil	*s*
anxiet*y*	*ies*
anxious	*ly*
any	*body, one, how, thing, way, where*

ap	
apart	
apartment	*s*
ape	*d, ȩing, s*
apiar*y*	*ies*
apiece	
apologetic	*al, ally*
apologize	*d, ȩing, s*
apolog*y*	*ies*
apostle	*s*
appal	*led, ling, lingly, s*
apparatus	*es* or **apparatus**
apparent	*ly*
appeal	*ed, ing, ingly, s*
appear	*ed, ing, ance, s*
appendicitis	
appetite	*s*
appetizing	*ly*
applaud	*ed, ing, s*
applause	
apple	*-core, -pie, -sauce, -tart, -tree, s*
appliance	*s*
applicant	*s*
application	*s*
apply	*ing*
appl*ied*	*ies*
appoint	*ed, ing, ment, s*
appreciate	*d, ȩing, s*
appreciation	
apprentice	*d, ȩing, ship, s*
approach	*ed, ing, es*
approval	
approve	*d, ȩing, s*
approximate	*ly, d, ȩing, s*
apricot	*s*
April	*-fool, s*
apron	*s*

ȩ Drop **e** before adding *ing*

aq   ar   as

aq

aquarium	*s* or **aquaria**
aquatic	*s*
aqueduct	*s*

ar

arable	
arc* (curve)	*-lamp, -light, s*
arcade	*s*
arch	*ed, ing, es*
archway	*s*
archaeological	*ly*
archaeologist	*s*
archaeology	
archer	*y, s*
architect	*ure, ural, s*
arctic	
are	
aren't (are not)	
area	*s*
arena	*s*
argue	*d, ∉ing, s*
argument	*ative, s*
arise	*n, ∉ing, s*
arithmetic	*al*
ark* (boat; box)	*s*
arm	*ed, ing, band, chair, ful, hole, pit, s*
armada	*s*
armament	*s*
armistice	*s*
armour	*ed, y, -plated, -plating*
arm *y*	*ies*
arose	
around	
arouse	*d, ∉ing, s*
arrange	*d, ∉ing, r, ment, s*

array	*ed, ing, s*
arrest	*ed, ing, s*
arrival	*s*
arrive	*d, ∉ing, s*
arrow	*-head, s*
arsenic	
art	*work, s*
artist	*ic, ically, s*
artful	*ly, ness*
arter *y*	*ies*
article	*s*
artificial	*ity, ly, ness*
artillery	*man, men*

as

ascend	*ed, ing, s*
ascent	*s*
ascertain	*ed, ing, s*
ash	*en, y, es*
ashamed	
ashore	
aside	
ask	*ed, ing, s*
asleep	
asparagus	
asphyxiate	*d, ∉ing, s*
aspirin	*s*
ass	*es*
assail	*ed, ing, ant, s*
assassin	*ation, s*
assassinate	*d, ∉ing, s*
assault	*ed, ing, s*
assemble	*d, ∉ing, s*
assembl *y*	*ies*
assist	*ed, ing, ance, s*
assistant	*s*

*∉ Drop **e** before adding *ing**

* arc
  ark

at   au av

associate	d, ∉ing, s
association	s
assort	ed, ing, ment, s
assume	d, ∉ing, s
assure	d, ∉ing, s
aster	s
asthma	tic, tical
astonish	ed, ing, es, ment
astound	ed, ing, s
astray	
astride	
astrologer	s
astrolog y	ical
astronaut	s
astronomer	s
astronom y	ical
asylum	s

at

ate* (eat)	
athlete	s
athletic	ally, s
Atlantic	
atlas	es
atmosphere	s
atom	ic, -bomb, s
atrocious	ly, ness
attach	ed, ing, able, es
attachment	s
attack	ed, ing, er, s
attain	ed, ing, able, ment, s
attempt	ed, ing, s
attend	ed, ing, ance, s
attendant	s
attention	s
attentive	ly, ness

attic	s
attitude	s
attract	ed, ing, ion, s
attractive	ly, ness
attribute	d, ∉ing, s

au

auburn	
auction	ed, ing, eer, s
audible	
audience	s
audition	ed, ing, s
August	s
aunt	s
auntie s or **aunt** y	ies
author	s
authoress	es
authorit y	ies
authorize	d, ∉ing, s
autobiograph y	ical, ies
autograph	ed, ing, s
automatic	ally
automation	
autumn	al, s

av

available	
avalanche	s
avenge	d, ∉ing, r, s
avenue	s
average	d, ∉ing, s
aviar y	ies
aviation	
aviator	s
avoid	ed, ing, able, ance, s

∉ Drop **e** before adding *ing*

* ate
  eight (8)

aw

await	ed, ing, s
awake	d, ȩing, s
awaken	ed, ing, s
award	ed, ing, s
aware	ness
away	
awe	some, struck, stricken
awful	ly, ness
awhile	
awkward	ly, ness
awning	s
awoke or **awaked**	
awry	

ax

axe	d, ȩing, -blade, -handle, s
ax is	es
axle	s

ba

babe	s
baboon	s
bab y	ies
bachelor	s
back	ed, ing, cloth, ground, yard, s
backward	ly, ness, s
bacon	
bad	-tempered, ly, ness
badge	s
badger	ed, ing, s
badminton	-racket
baffle	d, ȩing, s
bag	ged, ging, ful, -snatcher, s
baggage	

bagg y	ier, iest, ily, iness
bagpipe	s
bail* (wicket cross-piece)	s
bait	ed, ing, s
bake	d, ȩing, r, house, s
baker y	ies
balance	d, ȩing, r, s
balcon y	ies
bald	ing, er, est, ly, ness, -headed
bale* (bundle)	d, ȩing, r, s
bale* ⎰ out of plane or ⎱	d, ȩing, r, s
bail* ⎱ throw out water ⎰	ed, ing, er, s
ball*	-game, point, -pen, room, s
ballast	
ballerina	s
ballet	-dancing, -dancer, -shoe, s
balloon	ed, ing, ist, s
ballot	ed, ing, -paper, s
bamboo	s
ban	ned, ning, s
banana	s
band	ed, ing, sman, smen, stand, s
bandage	d, ȩing, s
bandit	s
bang	ed, ing, er, s
bangle	s
banish	ed, ing, es, ment
banister	s
banjo	es or s
bank	ed, ing, er, -book, note, s
bankrupt	ed, ing, s, cy
banner	s
banquet	ed, ing, s
bantam	s
baptism	s
baptize	d, ȩing, s
bar	red, ring, maid, s

ȩ Drop **e** before adding *ing*

*	bail	ball
	bale	bawl

be

barbecue	d, ∅ing, s
barbed	-wire
barber	s
bare* (naked; empty)	ly, ness, d, ∅ing, s
bargain	ed, ing, er, s
barge	d, ∅ing, e, -pole, s
bark	ed, ing, er, s
barley	corn, -sugar, -water, s
barn	-dance, -owl, yard, s
barnacle	s
barometer	s
baron* (lord)	et, s
barrack	ed, ing, er, -room, -square, s
barrel	ful, s
barren* (bare; empty)	ly, ness
barricade	d, ∅ing, s
barrier	s
barrister	s
barrow	-boy, s
barter	ed, ing, er, s
base	d, ∅ing, r, st, ly, less, ness, -line, s
baseball	s
basement	s
bash	ed, ing, es
bashful	ly, ness
basin	ful, s
bask	ed, ing, s
basket	ball, ful, s
bat	ted, ting, sman, smen, s
batch	es
bath	ed, ing, mat, robe, room, -water, s
bathe	d, ∅ing, r, s
bathing-costume	s
baton	s
battalion	s
batter	ed, ing, s
battery	ies

battle	d, ∅ing, axe, field, ship, s
bawl* (shout; cry out)	ed, ing, s
bay	-window, s
bayonet	ed, ing, s
bazaar	s

be

beach* (seashore)	ed, ing, es
beacon	s
bead	ed, ing, work, s
beak	s
beaker	s
beam	ed, ing, s
bean* (plant)	-bag, pole, stalk, s
bear* (carry; endure)	able, ing, er, s
bear* (animal)	skin, s
beard	ed, s
beast	s
beastly	ier, iest, iness
beat* (hit; defeat)	en, ing, er, s
beautiful	ly
beauty	ies
beaver	s
became	
because	
beckon	ed, ing, s
become	∅ing, s
bed	ded, ding, clothes, side, time, room, s
bee	hive, line, keeper, s
beech* (tree)	es
beef	burger, eater, steak, s
been* (past of be)	
beer	y, -barrel, -bottle, -can, s
beet* (vegetable)	root, s
beetle	s
before	hand

∅ Drop **e** before adding *ing*

*	bare	baron		bawl	beach	bean	beat
	bear	barren		ball	beech	been	beet

beg	*ged, ging, s*
beggar	*ly, s*
began	
begin	*ning, ner, s*
begun	
begone	
behave	*d, ėing, s*
behaviour	
behead	*ed, ing, s*
behind	*hand*
being	*s*
belief	*s*
believe	*d, ėing, r, s*
bell	*-ringer, -tent, -tower, s*
bellow	*ed, ing, er, s*
belong	*ed, ing, s*
below	
belt	*ed, ing, s*
bench	*es*
bend	*ing, er, s*
bent	
beneath	
benefit	*ed, ing, s*
benevolent	*ly*
beret* (cap)	*s*
berr *y** (fruit)	*ies*
berth* (bunk; moor a ship)	*ed, ing, s*
beside	*s*
besiege	*d, ėing, r, s*
best	*-seller*
bet	*ted, ting, ter, s*
betray	*al, ed, ing, er, s*
better	*ed, ing, s*
between	
beware	
bewilder	*ed, ing, ment, s*
beyond	

bi

Bible	*s*
bicker	*ed, ing, s*
bicycle	*d, ėing, -clip, -pump, s*
bid	*ding, der, s*
bide	*d, ėing, s*
big	*ger, gest, ness*
bike	*d, ėing, s*
bikini	*s*
bilberr *y*	*ies*
bilge	*-water, -pump, s*
bilious	*ly, ness*
bill	*ed, ing, s*
billet	*ed, ing, s*
billiard	*-ball, -cue, -room, -table, s*
billion	*s*
billow	*ed, ing, s*
bind	*ing, er, s*
bingo	*-hall, s*
binoculars	
biograph *y*	*ical, ies*
biolog *y*	*ical, ist*
biped	*s*
birch	*es*
bird	*-bath, -cage, -seed, -table, s*
birth* (born)	*day, mark, place, rate, s*
biscuit	*s*
bisect	*ed, ing, ion, s*
bishop	*s*
bison	**bison**
bit	*ty, s*
bitch	*es*
bite	*ėing, r, s*
bitten	
bitter	*er, est, ly, ness*
bittern	*s*
bivouac	*ked, king, s*

*ė Drop **e** before adding* ing

*	beret berth
	berry birth
	bury

10

bl   bo

bl

black	ed, ing, er, est, ness, smith, s
black	-beetle, bird, board, -currant, s
blackberry	ing
blackberr ied	ies
blacken	ed, ing, s
blackmail	ed, ing, er, s
blade	d, s
blame	d, ǿing, less, s
blancmange	s
blank	ed, ing, er, est, ly, ness, s
blanket	s
blare	d, ǿing, s
blast	ed, ing, s
blaze	d, ǿing, s
blazer	s
bleach	ed, ing, es
bleak	er, est, ly, ness
bleat	ed, ing, s
bleed	ing, s
bled	
blend	ed, ing, er, s
bless	ed, ing, ings, es
blew* (blow)	
blind	ed, ing, er, est, ly, ness, s
blindfold	ed, ing, s
blind-man's-buff	
blink	ed, ing, er, s
blister	ed, ing, s
blizzard	s
block	age, ed, ing, s
blockade	d, ǿing, s
blond (masc.)	er, est, s
blonde (fem.)	r, st, s
blood	hound, shed, -stained, thirsty, y
bloom	ed, ing, s
blossom	ed, ing, s

blot	ted, ting, ter, s
blouse	s
blow	n, ing, y, er, lamp, pipe, s
blue* (colour)	r, st, ness, bell, bottle, s
blunder	ed, ing, s
blunt	ed, ing, er, est, ly, ness, s
blush	ed, ing, es
bluster	ed, ing, y, s

bo

boar* (male pig)	s
board* (wood; ship; lodge)	ed, ing, s
boarder* (one who boards; lodger)	s
boast	ed, ing, er, s
boastful	ly, ness
boat	ed, ing, er, man, men, -race, s
bob	bed, bing, -sleigh, s
bod y	ies
bog	ged, ging, s
bogg y	ier, iest, iness
boil	ed, ing, er, s
boisterous	ly, ness
bold	er,* est, ly, ness
bolt	ed, ing, s
bomb	ed, ing, er, -proof, shell, sight, s
bombard	ed, ing, ment, s
bone	d, ǿing, ǿy, -dry, -idle, -shaker, s
bonfire	s
bonnet	s
bonn y	ier, iest, ily, iness
book	ed, ing, case, let, seller, stall, s
booking office	s
boom	ed, ing, s
boot	ed, ing, lace, s
border* (edge)	ed, ing, er, less, line, s
bore* (drill hole; weary)	d,* ǿing, dom, s

ǿ Drop **e** before adding *ing*

*	blew	boar	board	boarder	bolder
	blue	bore	bored	border	boulder

born* (birth)	
borne* (carried)	
borrow	*ed, ing, er, s*
boss	*ed, ing, es*
boss *y*	*ier, iest, ily, iness*
botan *y*	*ical, ist*
both	
bother	*ed, ing, some, s*
bottle	*d, ǿing, -opener, s*
bottom	*ed, ing, less, s*
bough* (branch)	*s*
bought (buy)	
boulder* (large rock)	*s*
bounce	*d, ǿing, r, s*
bound	*ed, ing, less, s*
boundar *y*	*ies*
bouquet	*s*
bow* (bend)	*ed, ing, s*
bow	*man, men, shot, string, -tie, s*
bowl	*ed, ing, er, s*
bowl	*ful, s*
box	*ed, ing, es*
boxer	*s*
Boxing Day	*s*
boy* (lad)	*ish, hood, -friend, s*
Boy Scout	*s*

br

brace	*d, ǿing, s*
bracelet	*s*
bracken	
bracket	*ed, ing, s*
brag	*ged, ging, gart, s*
braid	*ed, ing, s*
brain	*ed, ing, less, storm, wave, s*
brain *y*	*ier, iest, ily, iness*

brake* (to stop)	*d, ǿing, s*
bramble	*s*
branch	*ed, ing, es*
brand	*ed, ing, -new, s*
brandish	*ed, ing, es*
brand *y*	*ies*
brass	*es*
brave	*d, ǿing, r, st, ly, s*
bravery	
bravo	*s*
brawl	*ed, ing, er, s*
brawn	
brawn *y*	*ier, iest, iness*
brazen	*ed, ing, ly, ness*
brazier	*s*
bread*	*-bin, -board, -sauce, -crumb, s*
breadth	*s*
break*	*able, age, ing, er, -down, water, s*
breakfast	*ed, ing, -table, -room, s*
breast	*ed, ing, plate, -stroke, s*
breath	*less, lessly, -taking, s*
breathe	*d, ǿing, r, s*
bred* (brought-up)	
breed	*ing, er, s*
breeze	*s*
breez *y*	*ier, iest, ily, iness*
brew	*ed, ing, er, s*
brewer *y*	*ies*
bribe	*d, ǿing, ry, s*
brick	*ed, ing, laying, layer, work, yard, s*
bridal* (of a bride, wedding)	*-gown*
bride	*groom, smaid, s*
bridge	*d, ǿing, head, s*
bridle* (horse's headgear)	*-path, road, s*
brief	*ed, ing, er, est, ly, ness, case, s*
brigade	*s*
brigand	*s*

*ǿ Drop **e** before adding ing*

bright	er, est, ly, ness
brighten	ed, ing, s
brilliance	
brilliant	ly
brim	med, ming, ful, s
bring	ing, s
brink	s
brisk	er, est, ly, ness
bristle	d, ǿing, s
bristly	ier, iest, iness
brittle	ness
broad	er, est, ly, -minded, side, s
broaden	ed, ing, s
broadcast	ing, er, s
brocade	s
broccoli	
broke	
broken	-down, -hearted
bronchitis	
bronze	d, ǿing, s
brooch	es
brood	ed, ing, y, s
brook	s
broom	stick, s
broth	s
brother	ly, s
brother(s)**-in-law**	
brought (bring)	
brow	s
brown	ed, ing, er, est, ish, ness, s
brownie	s
bruise	d, ǿing, r, s
brunette	s
brush	ed, ing, es
Brussels sprouts	
brutal	ity, ly
brute	s

bu

bubble	d, ǿing, -bath, -gum, s
bubbly	ier, iest, iness
buccaneer	s
buck	ed, ing, skin, s
bucket	ful, s
buckle	d, ǿing, s
bud	ded, ding, s
budge	d, ǿing, s
budgerigar	s
budget	ed, ing, s
buffalo	es or **buffalo**
buffer	s
buffet	ed, ing, s
bugle	-call, r, s
build	ing, er, s
built	
bulb	s
bulge	d, ǿing, s
bulk	
bulky	ier, iest, ily, iness
bull	dog, fight, frog, ring, -terrier, s
bull's-eye	s
bulldoze	d, ǿing, r, s
bullet	-hole, -proof, -wound, s
bulletin	s
bullion	
bullock	s
bully	ing
bullied	ies
bulrush	es
bumble-bee	s
bump	ed, ing, er, s
bumpy	ier, iest, ily, iness
bunch	ed, ing, es
bundle	d, ǿing, s
bung	ed, ing, -hole, s

ǿ Drop **e** before adding *ing*

bungalow	s
bungle	d, e̷ing, r, s
bunk	s
bunker	ed, ing, s
Bunsen burner	s
bunting	
buoy* (floating marker)	ant, ed, ing, s
burden	ed, ing, some, s
bureau	x or s
burglar	-alarm, s
burglar y	ies
burgle	d, e̷ing, s
burial	-ground, -place, s
burl y	ier, iest, ily, iness
burn	ed, ing, er, s
burnt or **burned**	
burrow	ed, ing, er, s
burst	ing, s
bury* (cover)	ing
bur ied	ies
bus	man, men, es
busb y	ies
bush	es
bush y	ier, iest, ily, iness
business	man, men, es
bustle	d, e̷ing, r, s
busy	ing, ness
bus ied	ier, iest, ily, ies
butcher	ed, ing, s
butler	s
butter	ed, ing, scotch, cup, s
butterfl y	ies
button	ed, ing, -hole, s
buy* (purchase)	ing, er, s
buzz	ed, ing, es
buzzer	s
buzzard	s

by

by* (near to, etc.)	
bye* (a run)	s
bygone	s
by-pass	ed, ing, es
bystander	s
byway	s

ca

cabaret	s
cabbage	s
cabin	-boy, s
cabinet	-maker, s
cable	d, e̷ing, gram, -car, s
cackle	d, e̷ing, r, s
cactus	es or **cacti**
caddie* (golfer's club-carrier)	d, s
caddying	
cadd y* (tea box)	ies
cadet	s
cadge	d, e̷ing, r, s
café	s
cafeteria	s
cage	d, e̷ing, s
cake	d, e̷ing, s
calamit y	ies
calculate	d, e̷ing, s
calculation	s
calculator	s
calendar	s
calf	skin, **calves**
call	ed, ing, er, s
calm	ed, ing, er, est, ly, ness, s
came	
camel	-hair, s
camera	man, men, s
camouflage	d, e̷ing, s

e̷ Drop **e** before adding *ing*

*	buoy	bury	buy	caddie
	boy	beret	bye	caddy
		berry	by	

camp	*ed, ing, er, -bed, -fire, site, s*	**career**	*ed, ing, s*
campaign	*ed, ing, er, s*	**caress**	*ed, ing, es*
canal	*s*	**cargo**	*es*
canary	*ies*	**caricature**	*d, ǿing, s*
cancel	*led, ling, lation, s*	**carnation**	*s*
candidate	*s*	**carnival**	*s*
candle	*-light, wick, stick, s*	**carnivorous**	
candy	*ied, ies*	**carol**	*led, ling, ler, -singer, s*
cane	*d, ǿing, s*	**carpenter**	*s*
cannibal	*ism, s*	**carpentry**	
cannon	*ed, -ball, -shot, s* or **cannon**	**carpet**	*ed, ing, -sweeper, s*
cannot		**carriage**	*way, s*
can't (cannot)		**carrot**	*s*
canoe	*d, ing, ist, s*	**carry**	*ing*
canteen	*s*	**carr**ied	*ies*
canter	*ed, ing, s*	**carrier**	*-bag, -pigeon, s*
canvas* (strong cloth)	*es*	**cart**	*ed, ing, -load, -horse, -wheel, s*
canvass* (seek votes, orders)	*ed, ing, es*	**carton**	*s*
canyon	*s*	**cartoon**	*ed, ing, ist, s*
capable	*y*	**cartridge**	*-belt, -case, s*
cape	*s*	**carve**	*d, ǿing, r, s*
capital	*s*	**cascade**	*d, ǿing, s*
capsize	*d, ǿing, s*	**case**	*s*
capsule	*s*	**cash**	*ed, ing, -box, es*
captain	*ed, ing, s*	**cashier**	*s*
captive	*s*	**cask**	*s*
captivity	*ies*	**casket**	*s*
capture	*d, ǿing, s*	**casserole**	*d, ǿing, s*
car	*-load, -park, port, s*	**cassette**	*-player, -recorder, s*
caramel	*s*	**cast**	*ing, s*
caravan	*ned, ning, ner, s*	**castaway**	*s*
carcasses or **carcase**	*s*	**castle**	*s*
card	*board, -game, -room, -table, s*	**castor oil**	
cardigan	*s*	**casual**	*ly, ness, s*
care	*d, ǿing, free, taker, s*	**casualt**y	*ies*
careful	*ly, ness*	**catalogue**	*d, ǿing, s*
careless	*ly, ness*	**catapult**	*ed, ing, s*

ǿ Drop **e** before adding *ing*

*   canvas
     canvass

ce

catastrophe	s
catch	ing, es
catch y	ier, iest, iness
cater	ed, ing, er, s
caterpillar	s
cathedral	s
Catherine wheel	s
Catholic	s
catkin	s
cattle	-market, -shed, -show, -truck
caught	
cauldron	s
cauliflower	s
cause	d, ęing, s
caution	ed, ing, s
cautious	ly, ness
cavalier	s
cavalry	
cave	d, ęing, -man, -men, -dweller, s
cavern	s
cavit y	ies

ce

cease	d, ęing, less, lessly, s
cedar	s
ceiling* (roof of room)	s
celandine	s
celebrate	d, ęing, s
celebration	s
celebrit y	ies
celery	
cell* (small room)	s
cellar* (underground room)	s
cello	s
cellophane	
cement	ed, ing, -mixer, s

ch a

cemeter y	ies
cent* (coin)	s
centigrade	
centimetre	s
central	ly
centre	d, ęing, -forward, -piece, s
centur y	ies
cereal* (wheat, oats, etc.)	s
ceremon y	ies
certain	ly, ty
certificate	s

ch

chaffinch	es
chain	ed, ing, -mail, -saw, -store, s
chair	ed, ing, man, woman, -lift, s
chalet	s
chalk	ed, ing, s
chalk y	ier, iest, iness
challenge	d, ęing, r, s
chamber	maid, s
chamois	-leather
champagne	s
champion	ed, ing, ship, s
chance	d, ęing, s
chandelier	s
change	able, d, ęing, s
channel	led, ling, s
chant	ed, ing, s
chaos	
chaotic	ally
chapel	s
chapter	s
char	red, ring, woman, women, s
character	istic, s
charade	s

ę Drop e before adding ing

*	ceiling	cell	cellar	cent	cereal
	sealing	sell	seller	sent	serial
				scent	

charcoal	
charge	d, ¢ing, r, s
chariot	eer, s
charit y	ies
charm	ed, ing, er, s
chart	ed, ing, room, s
charter	ed, ing, s
chase	d, ¢ing, r, s
chasm	s
chat	ted, ting, s
chatter	ed, ing, er, s
chatt y	ier, iest, ily, iness
chauffeur	s
cheap	er, est, ly, ness
cheapen	ed, ing, s
cheat	ed, ing, er, s
check*	ed, ing, er, -list, -out, -point, s
check* (pattern)	ed, s
cheek	ed, ing, -bone, s
cheek y	ier, iest, ily, iness
cheer	ed, ing, -leader, s
cheerful	ly, ness
cheerless	ly, ness
cheer y	ier, iest, ily, iness
cheese	burger, cake, cloth, -straw, s
chef	s
chemical	ly, s
chemist	s
chemistry	
cheque* (money-order)	-book, s
cherish	ed, ing, es
cherr y	ies
chess	-board, -piece, -man, -men
chest	s
chestnut	-tree, s
chew	ed, ing, y, er, s
chewing-gum	

chick	weed, s
chicken	-feed, -wire, s or **chicken**
chicken-pox	
chief	ly, tain, s
chilblain	s
child	ish, hood, like, less, **children**
chill	ed, ing, er, s
chill y	ier, iest, ily, iness
chime	d, ¢ing, s
chimney	-pot. -stack, -sweep, s
chimpanzee	s
chin	-strap, s
china	-shop, ware
chink	ed, ing, s
chintz	es
chip	ped, ping, per, s
chirp	ed, ing, s
chirp y	ier, iest, ily, iness
chisel	led, ling, s
chivalrous	ly
chivalry	
chlorine	
chloroform	ed, ing, s
chocolate	s
choice	r, st, ly, ness, s
choir* (of singers)	-boy, -master, s
choke	d, ¢ing, s
choose	¢ing, s
chose	n
chop	ped, ping, per, s
chopstick	s
chorus	ed, ing, es
chow	, s
christen	ed, ing, s
Christ	
Christian	ity, s
Christmas	-box, es, -time, -tree, sy

¢ Drop **e** before adding *ing*

*	check	choir
	cheque	quire

chromium	-plated, -plating
chrysalis	es
chrysanthemum	s
chubb y	ier, iest, ily, iness
chuckle	d, ǿing, s
chug	ged, ging, s
chum	med, ming, s
chumm y	ier, iest, ily, iness
chunk	s
church	es
churchyard	s
churn	ed, ing, s
chute* (a slide)	s
chutney	s

ci

cider or **cyder**	s
cigar	-case, -holder, -lighter, s
cigarette	-case, -holder, -lighter, s
cinder	-path, -track, s
cine-	camera, film, projector
cinema	-goer, s
circle	d, ǿing, s
circular	s
circulate	d, ǿing, s
circulation	s
circumference	s
circumstance	s
circus	es
cistern	s
citizen	s
cit y	ies
civil	ity, ly
civilian	s
civilization	s
civilize	d, ǿing, s

cl

claim	ed, ing, s
clamber	ed, ing, s
clamm y	ier, iest, ily, iness
clamp	ed, ing, s
clang	ed, ing, s
clank	ed, ing, s
clap	ped, ping, per, s
clash	ed, ing, es
clasp	ed, ing, s
class	ed, ing, es, rooms
classic	al, s
clatter	ed, ing, s
claw	ed, ing, s
clay	ey, -pigeon, -pipe, -pit, s
clean	ed, ing, er, est, ly, ness, s
cleanliness	
cleanse	d, ǿing, r, s
clear	ed, ing, er, est, ly, ness, s
clench	ed, ing, es
clergy	man, men
clerk	s
clever	er, est, ly, ness
click	ed, ing, s
client	s
cliff	-top, s
climate	s
climb	ed, ing, er, s
cling	ing, s
clinic	al, ally, s
clink	ed, ing, er, s
clip	ped, ping, per, s
cloak	ed, ing, room, s
clock	ed, ing, wise, work, -tower, s
cloister	ed, ing, s
close (shut)	d, ǿing, s
close (near; stuffy)	r, st, ly, ness

ǿ Drop e before adding ing

* chute
  shoot

CO_a   cob   coc   cod   cof   coi   col   com

cloth s	**code** d, *ẹing*, s
clothe d, *ẹing*, s	**coffee** -bar, -bean, -cup, -pot, -table, s
clothes -basket, -horse, -line, -peg	**coffin** s
cloud ed, ing, less, lessly, burst, s	**coil** ed, ing, s
cloudy ier, iest, ily, iness	**coin** age, ed, ing, s
clover s	**coincide** d, *ẹing*, s
clown ed, ing, s	**coincidence** s
club bed, bing, house, room, s	**cold** er, est, ish, ly, ness, -storage, s
cluck ed,ing, s	**collapse** d, *ẹing*, s
clue less, s	**collapsible**
clump ed, ing, s	**collar** -bone, -stud, s
clumsy ier, iest, ily, iness	**collect** ed, ing, ion, or, s
clung	**college** s
cluster ed, ing, s	**collide** d, *ẹing*, s
clutch ed, ing, es	**collision** s
clutter ed, ing, s	**collie** s
	collier s
	colliery ies
	colonel* (officer) s
co	**colonize** d, *ẹing*, s
coach man, men, ed, ing, es	**colon**y ies
coal man, men, -mine, -miner, s	**colossal** ly
coarse* (rough) r, st, ly, ness	**colour** ed, ing, ful, less, -scheme, s
coast al, ed, ing, line, guard, s	**column** s
coat ed, ing, -hanger, s	**comb** ed, ing, s
coax ed, ing, es	**combat** ed, ing, s
cobble d, *ẹing*, r, -stone, s	**combination** s
cobra s	**combine** d, *ẹing*, -harvester, s
cobweb by, s	**come** *ẹing*, s
cock ed, ing, -fight, pit, tail, s	**comedian** (masc.) s
cockatoo s	**comedienne** (fem.) s
cockerel s	**comed**y ies
cockle -shell, s	**comet** s
cockney s	**comfort** able, ably, ed, ing, s
cockroach es	**comic** al, ally, s
cocoa	**command** ed, ing, er, ment, s
coconut -matting, -milk, -palm, s	**commemorate** d, *ẹing*, s
cocoon s	

ẹ Drop **e** before adding *ing*

commence	*d, ȩing, ment, s*
comment	*ed, ing, ator, s*
commentary	*ies*
commerce	
commercial	*s*
commission	*ed, ing, aire, er, s*
commit	*ted, ting, ment, s*
committee	*-room, s*
common	*er, est, ly, ness, -room, s*
commotion	*s*
communicate	*d, ȩing, s*
communication	*s*
communion	
community	*ies*
compact	*s*
companion	*ship, s*
company	*ies*
comparative	*ly, s*
compare	*d, ȩing, s*
comparison	*s*
compartment	*s*
compass	*es*
compel	*led, ling, s*
compete	*d, ȩing, s*
competition	*s*
competitor	*s*
complain	*ed, ing, s*
complaint	*s*
complete	*d, ȩing, ly, ness, s*
complexion	*s*
complicate	*d, ȩing, s*
compliment	*ed, ing, ary, s*
compose	*d, ȩing, r, s*
composition	*s*
comprehensive school	*s*
computer	*s*
comrade	*ship, s*

conceal	*ed, ing, ment, s*
conceit	*ed, edly*
concentrate	*d, ȩing, s*
concentration	
concern	*ed, ing, s*
concert	*s*
conclude	*d, ȩing, s*
conclusion	*s*
concrete	*d, ȩing, s*
condemn	*ed, ing, ation, s*
condition	*ed, ing, er, s*
conduct	*ed, ing, or, s*
conductress	*es*
conference	*s*
confess	*ed, ing, es*
confession	*s*
confetti	
confide	*d, ȩing, s*
confidence	
confident	*ial, ially, ly*
confirm	*ed, ing, ation, s*
confiscate	*d, ȩing, s*
confuse	*d, ȩing, s*
confusion	*s*
congratulate	*d, ȩing, s*
congratulation	*s*
congregate	*d, ȩing, s*
congregation	*s*
conjure	*d, ȩing, s*
conjurer or **conjuror**	*s*
conker* (horse-chestnut)	*s*
connect	*ed, ing, ion, s*
conquer* (defeat)	*ed, ing, or, s*
conquest	*s*
conscience	*-smitten, s*
conscientious	*ly, ness*
conscious	*ly, ness*

ȩ Drop **e** before adding *ing*

* conker
conquer

consent	*ed, ing, s*	**cook**	*ed, ing, er, ery, book, house, s*
consequence	*s*	**cool**	*ed, ing, er, est, ish, ly, ness, s*
consequent	*ly*	**co-operate**	*d, ∉ing, s*
conservative	*s*	**co-operation**	
consider	*ed, ing, able, ably, ate, ation, s*	**copper**	*s*
consist	*ed, ing, s*	**coppice** or **copse**	*s*
consolation	*-prize, s*	**copy**	*ing*
conspicuous	*ly, ness*	**cop**ied	*ies*
constable	*s*	**coral**	*-island, -reef, s*
constant	*ly*	**cord**	*s*
construct	*ed, ing, ion, or, s*	**cordial**	*s*
consult	*ed, ing, ation, s*	**cordon**	*ed, ing, s*
consume	*d, ∉ing, r, s*	**corduroy**	*s*
contact	*ed, ing, s*	**core*** (middle of apple, etc.)	*d, ∉ing, s*
contain	*ed, ing, er, s*	**corgi**	*s*
.**contemporar**y	*ies*	**cork**	*ed, ing, screw, s*
content	*ed, ing, ment, s*	**corn**	*-cob, field, flake, s*
contest	*ed, ing, ant, s*	**corned beef**	
continent	*al, s*	**corner**	*ed, ing, s*
continual	*ly*	**cornet**	*s*
continue	*d, ∉ing, s*	**coronation**	*s*
continuation		**corporal**	*s*
continuous	*ly, ness*	**corporation**	*s*
contradict	*ed, ing, ion, s*	**corps*** (group of cadets, etc.) **corps**	
contribute	*d, ∉ing, s*	**corpse**	*s*
contribution	*s*	**correct**	*ed, ing, ion, ly, ness, s*
control	*led, ling, ler, -column, -lever, s*	**correspond**	*ed, ing, ence, ent, s*
convalesce	*d, ∉ing, nce, nt, s*	**corridor**	*s*
convenience	*s*	**cosmetic**	*s*
convenient	*ly*	**cosmonaut**	*s*
convent	*s*	**cost**	*ing, s*
conversation	*s*	**costl**y	*ier, iest, iness*
convert	*ed, ing, s*	**coster**	*monger, s*
convey	*ed, ing, ance, s*	**costume**	*s*
convict	*ed, ing, ion, s*	**cos**y	*ier, iest, ily, iness, ies*
convince	*d, ∉ing, s*	**cottage**	*s*
convoy	*ed, ing, s*	**cotton**	*wool, s*

∉ Drop **e** before adding *ing*

*   core

*   corps

couch	*es*	**crank**	*ed, ing, s*
cough *ed, ing, er, -drop, -mixture, s*		**crash**	*ed, ing, es*
could		**crate**	*d, ¢ing, ful, s*
couldn't (could not)		**crater**	*s*
council *lor, -chamber, -house, s*		**crave**	*d, ¢ing, s*
count *ed, ing, er, less, -down, s*		**crawl**	*ed, ing, er, s*
counter *ed, ing, -attack, foil, s*		**crayon**	*ed, ing, s*
countess	*es*	**craze**	*d, ¢ing, s*
country	*ies*	**craz**y	*ier, iest, ily, iness*
county	*ies*	**creak*** (noise)	*ed, ing, s*
couple	*d, ¢ing, s*	**creak**y	*ier, iest, ily, iness*
coupon	*s*	**cream** *ed, ing, er, -cake, -cheese, s*	
courage		**cream**y	*ier, iest, ily, iness*
courageous	*ly, ness*	**crease**	*d, ¢ing, s*
course* (track; direction; of course) *s*		**create**	*d, ¢ing, s*
court *ed, ing, ier, room, ship, yard, s*		**creature**	*s*
courtesy	*ies*	**credit**	*able, ed, ing, or, s*
cousin	*ly, s*	**creek*** (small bay, sea-coast inlet)	*s.*
cove	*s*	**creep**	*ing, er, s*
cover	*ed, ing, s*	**creep**y	*ier, iest, ily, iness*
cow *boy, hand, herd, hide, shed, s*		**cremate**	*d, ¢ing, s*
coward	*s*	**crematorium**	*s*
cowardice		**creosote**	*d, ¢ing, s*
cowardly	*iness*	**crept**	
cowslip	*s*	**crescent**	*s*
		crest	*ed, ing, fallen, s*
		crevice	*s*
cr		**crew**	*ed, ing, s*
crab	*-apple, -pot, s*	**crib**	*bed, bing, ber, s*
crack	*ed, ing, er, s*	**cricket**	*ing, er, -field, s*
crackle	*d, ¢ing, s*	**cried**	
cradle	*d, ¢ing, s*	**crier**	*s*
craft	*sman, smen, s*	**cries**	
crafty	*ier, iest, ily, iness*	**crime**	*s*
cram	*med, ming, mer, s*	**criminal**	*s*
cramp	*ed, ing, s*	**crimson**	*ed, ing, s*
crane	*d, ¢ing, -driver, s*	**cringe**	*d, ¢ing, s*

¢ Drop **e** before adding *ing*

*   course   creak
     coarse   creek

crinkle	d, øing, s	**crumple**	d, øing, s
crinkly	ier, iest, iness	**crunch**	ed, ing, es
cripple	d, øing, s	**crusade**	d, øing, r, s
crisp	ed, ing, er, est, ly, ness, s	**crush**	ed, ing, es
crispy	ier, iest, ily, iness	**crust**	s
critic	al, ally, ism, s	**crust**y	ier, iest, ily, iness
criticize	d, øing, s	**crutch**	es
croak	ed, ing, er, s	**cry**	ing
croaky	ier, iest, ily, iness	**cr**ied	ies
crochet	ed, ing, -hook, s	**crypt**	s
crockery		**crystal**	s
crocodile	s		
crocus	es		
crook	s	**cu**	
crooked	ly, ness	**Cub Scout**	s
crop	ped, ping, per, s	**cube**	d, øing, s
croquet		**cubicle**	s
cross	ed, ing, er, est, ly, ness, es	**cuckoo**	-clock, s
crossroad	s	**cucumber**	s
crossword	s	**cuddle**	d, øing, some, s
crouch	ed, ing, es	**cue*** (hint; billiard-stick)	s
crow	ed, ing, bar, s	**cuff**	-link, s
crowd	ed, ing, s	**cul-de-sac**	**culs-de-sac**
crown	ed, ing, s	**culprit**	s
crucify	ing	**cultivate**	d, øing, s
crucified	ies	**cultivation**	
crucifix	es	**cunning**	ly
crucifixion	s	**cup**	ful, s
crude	r, st, ly, ness	**cupboard**	s
cruel	ler, lest, ly	**curate**	s
cruelty	ies	**curator**	s
cruet	s	**curb*** (hold back)	ed, ing, s
cruise	d, øing, r, s	**curdle**	d, øing, s
crumb	s	**cure**	d, øing, s
crumble	d, øing, s	**curio**	s
crumbly	ier, iest, iness	**curiosit**y	ies
crumpet	s	**curious**	ly, ness

ø Drop **e** before adding *ing*

*	cue	curb
	queue	kerb

curl	ed, ing, er, s
curly	ier, iest, ily, iness
currant* (fruit)	-bread, -bun, -cake, s
current* (flow of water, air, etc.)	s
curry	ied, ies
curse	d, ∅ing, s
curt	ly, ness
curtain	ed, ing, s
curtsy	ing
curtsied	ies
curve	d, ∅ing, s
cushion	s
custard	-powder, -pie, s
custom	s
customer	s
cut	ting, ter, -price, -rate, -throat, s
cutlass	es
cutlery	

cy

cycle	d, ∅ing, -clip, s
cyclist	s
cyclone	s
cygnet* (young swan)	s
cylinder	s
cymbal	ist, s
cypress	es

da

dab	bed, bing, ber, s
dabble	d, ∅ing, r, s
dachshund	s
dad	s
daddy	ies
daffodil	s

daft	er, est, ly, ness
dagger	s
dahlia	s
daily	ies
dainty	ier, iest, ily, iness, ies
dairy	ies
daisy	ies
dale	s
Dalmatian	s
dam	med, ming, s
damage	d, ∅ing, s
dame	s
damp	ed, ing, er, est, ly, ness, s
dampen	ed, ing, er, s
damson	-tree, s
dance	d, ∅ing, r, -band, -floor, s
dandelion	s
danger	s
dangerous	ly
dangle	d, ∅ing, s
dank	er, est, ly, ness
dapple	d, ∅ing, -grey, s
dare	d, ∅ing, -devil, s
dark	er, est, ly, ness
darken	ed, ing, s
darling	s
darn	ed, ing, er, s
dart	ed, ing, -board, s
dash	ed, ing, es
date	d, ∅ing, -stamp, -palm, s
daub	ed, ing, er, s
daughter	s
dawdle	d, ∅ing, r, s
dawn	ed, ing, s
day	break, dream, light, time, s
daze	d, ∅ing, s
dazzle	d, ∅ing, r, s

∅ Drop **e** before adding *ing*

de

de

dead	-beat, -end, -heat, line, lock, ness
deaden	ed, ing, er, s
deadly	ier, iest, iness
deaf	-aid, er, est, ly, ness
deafen	ed, ing, s
deal	ing, er, s
dealt	
dear* (beloved; costly)	er, est, ly, ness, s
death	ly, -bed, -blow, -rate, -ray, -trap, s
debate	d, ǿing, r, s
debris	
debt	or, s
decay	ed, ing, s
deceit	ful, fully, s
deceive	d, ǿing, r, s
December	s
decent	ly
decide	d, dly, ǿing, s
decimal	s
decipher	ed, ing, s
decision	s
deck	ed, ing, -chair, s
declare	d, ǿing, s
decline	d, ǿing, s
decorate	d, ǿing, s
decoration	s
decorator	s
decrease	d, ǿing, s
deduct	ed, ing, ion, s
deed	s
deep	er, est, ly, ness
deepen	ed, ing, s
deer* (animal)	skin, stalker, -park, **deer**
defeat	ed, ing, s
defect	ive, s
defence	less, lessly, s

defend	ed, ing, er, s
defiant	ly
definite	ly
degree	s
delay	ed, ing, s
deliberate	ly, ness, d, ǿing, s
delicacy	ies
delicate	ly, ness
delicious	ly, ness
delight	ed, ing, s
delightful	ly, ness
deliver	ed, ing, ance, s
delivery	ies
deluge	d, ǿing, s
demand	ed, ing, s
demolish	ed, ing, es
demon	s
demonstrate	d, ǿing, s
demonstration	s
demonstrator	s
dense	r, st, ly, ness
dent	ed, ing, s
dentist	s
deny	ing
denied	ies
depart	ed, ing, ure, s
department	s
depend	ed, ing, able, ent, s
deport	ed, ing, ation, s
deposit	ed, ing, or, s
depot	s
depth	-charge, s
deputy	ies
derail	ed, ing, ment, s
derelict	s
descant	-recorder, s
descend	ed, ing, ant, s

ǿ Drop **e** before adding *ing*

* dear
* deer

di

descent	s	**di**		
describe	d, ẹing, s	diagram	s
description	s	dial	led, ling, ler, s
desert (sandy place)	s	dialect	s
desert* (run away)	ed, ing, ion, er, s	dialogue	s
deserve	d, ẹing, s	diameter	s
design	ed, ing, er, s	diamond	s
desire	d, ẹing, s	diary	ies
desk	s	dictate	d, ẹing, s
desolate	d, ẹing, ly, ness, s	dictation	s
despair	ed, ing, ingly, s	dictionary	ies
despatch or dispatch	ed, ing, es	didn't (did not)	
desperate	ly, ness	die* (small spotted cube)	**dice**
desperation		die* (lose life)	s
despise	d, ẹing, s	died* (lost life)	
despite		dying* (losing life)	
dessert* (fruit, pudding, etc.)	-spoon, s	diet	ed, ing, ician, s
destination	s	differ	ed, ing, ence, s
destroy	ed, ing, er, s	different	ly
destruction		difficult	
destructive	ly, ness	difficulty	ies
detach	ed, ing, es	dig	ging, ger, s
detail	ed, ing, s	digest	ed, ing, ion, ive, s
detain	ed, ing, s	dignify	ied, ies
detect	ed, ing, ion, or, s	dignity	
detective	s	dike or dyke	s
detention	s	dilapidated	
determination		dilute	d, ẹing, s
determine	d, ẹing, s	dim	med, ming, mer, mest, ly, ness, s
detest	able, ed, ing, s	dimension	s
develop	ed, ing, er, ment, s	dimple	d, ẹing, s
device	s	dine	d, ẹing, r, s
devil	ish, ry, ment, s	dining	-car, -hall, -room, -table
devise	d, ẹing, s	dinghy	ies
devote	d, ẹing, s	dingy	ier, iest, ily, iness
devour	ed, ing, er, s	dinner	-hour, -service, -table, -time, s
dew* (moisture)	y, -drop, -fall, -pond, s	dinosaur	s

ẹ Drop **e** before adding *ing*

*	desert	dew	die	died	dying
	dessert	due	dye	dyed	dyeing
		Jew			

dip	*ped, ping, per, s*	**dismal**	*ly, ness*
diploma	*s*	**dismantle**	*d, øing, s*
direct	*ed, ing, ly, ness, ive, or, s*	**dismay**	*ed, ing, s*
direction	*-finder, s*	**dismiss**	*ed, ing, es*
director *y*	*ies*	**dismount**	*ed, ing, s*
dirt	*-track*	**disobedience**	
dirt *ied*	*ier, iest, ily, iness, ies*	**disobedient**	*ly*
dirty	*ing*	**disobey**	*ed, ing, s*
disable	*d, øing, ment, s*	**disorder**	*ly, s*
disadvantage	*s*	**dispatch** or **despatch**	*ed, ing, es*
disagree	*able, d, ing, ment, s*	**dispensar** *y*	*ies*
disappear	*ed, ing, ance, s*	**dispense**	*d, øing, r, s*
disappoint	*ed, ing, ment, s*	**display**	*ed, ing, s*
disarm	*ed, ing, ament, s*	**displease**	*d, øing, s*
disarrange	*d, øing, ment, s*	**dispute**	*d, øing, s*
disaster	*s*	**disqualify**	*ing*
disastrous	*ly*	**disqualif** *ied*	*ies, ication*
disc or **disk**	*s*	**dissatisfy**	*ing*
discharge	*d, øing, s*	**dissatisf** *ied*	*ies, action*
disciple	*s*	**dissolve**	*d, øing, s*
discipline	*d, øing, s*	**distance**	*s*
discontent	*ed, edly, ment, s*	**distant**	*ly*
discothèque or **disco**	*-club, -dancing, s*	**distinct**	*ion, ive, ly, ness*
discourage	*d, øing, ment, s*	**distinguish**	*able, ed, ing, es*
discover	*ed, ing, er, s*	**distract**	*ed, ing, ion, s*
discover *y*	*ies*	**distress**	*ed, ing, es*
discuss	*ed, ing, es*	**disribute**	*d, øing, s*
discussion	*s*	**district**	*s*
disease	*d, s*	**disturb**	*ed, ing, ance, s*
disgrace	*d, øing, s*	**ditch**	*ed, ing, es*
disgraceful	*ly, ness*	**divan**	*s*
disguise	*d, øing, s*	**dive**	*d, øing, r, s*
disgust	*ed, ing, s*	**divert**	*ed, ing, s*
dish	*ed, ing, es*	**divide**	*d, øing, r, s*
dishearten	*ed, ing, s*	**division**	*s*
dishonest	*ly, y*	**divorce**	*d, øing, e, s*
dislike	*able, d, øing, s*	**dizz** *y*	*ier, iest, ily, iness*

ø Drop **e** before adding *ing*

do   dr

do	
docile	ly
dock	ed, ing, er, yard, s
doctor	' s
document	ed, ing, s'
dodge	d, ɇing, r, s
doe* (female animal)	s
does	
doesn't (does not)	
doing	s
dole	d, ɇing, ful, fully, s
doll	s
dollar	s
dolphin	s
domestic	ally, s
domesticate	d, ɇing, s
domino	es
donate	d, ɇing, s
donation	s
done	
donkey	s
don't (do not)	
doom	ed, ing, sday, s
door	bell, keeper, mat, step, way, s
dormitor y	ies
dose	d, ɇing, s
dot	ted, ting, s
double	d, ɇing, -jointed, -decker, s
doubt	ed, ing, less, er, s
doubtful	ly, ness
dough* (moist flour)	boy, nut, y
douse or **dowse**	d, ɇing, s
dove	cote, s
dowd y	ier, iest, ily, iness
down	stairs, hill, fall, pour, ward, s
doze	d, ɇing, s
dozen	s or **dozen**

dr	
drab	ber, best, ly, ness
drag	ged, ging, -net, s
dragon	s
dragonfl y	ies
drain	age, ed, ing, -pipe, s
drake	s
drama	tic, tist, s
dramatize	d, ɇing, s
drank	
drape	d, ɇing, s
draper	s
draper y	ies
drastic	ally
draught	sman, smen, -board, s
draught y	ier, iest, ily, iness
draw	n, ing, er, s
drawbridge	s
drawer	s
drawing	-board, -paper, -pin, -room, s
dread	ed, ing, s
dreadful	ly, ness
dream	ed, ing, land, like, er, s
dreamt or **dreamed**	
dream y	ier, iest, ily, iness
drear y	ier, iest, ily, iness
dredge	d, ɇing, r, s
drench	ed, ing, es
dress	ed, ing, es
dresser	s
dressing	-gown, -case, -room, -table, s
dressmaker	s
drew	
dribble	d, ɇing, r, s
drift	ed, ing, er, s
drill	ed, ing, er, s
drink	able, ing, er, s

ɇ Drop **e** before adding *ing*

* doe
    dough

du   dw   dy

drip	ped, ping, s
drive	ǿing, r, way, s
driven	
drivel	led, ling, ler, s
drizzle	d, ǿing, s
drizzl y	ier, iest, iness
dromedar y	ies
drone	d, ǿing, s
droop	ed, ing, s
drop	ped, ping, per, let, s
drought	s
drove	
drown	ed, ing, s
drowse	d, ǿing, s
drows y	ier, iest, ily, iness
drudgery	
drug	ged, ging, gist, -addict, store, s
drum	med, ming, mer, -major, stick, s
drunk	ard, s
drunken	ly, ness
dry	ing, ness
dr ied	ier, iest, ies
dryer or **drier** (noun)	s
dryly or **drily**	

du

dual* (two; double)	
duchess	es
duck	ed, ing, ling, s
due* (expected; owing)	s
duel* (a fight)	led, ling, list, s
duet	s
duffel or **duffle**	-bag, -coat, s
dug	-out
duke	dom, s
dull	ed, ing, er, est, ish, y, ness, s

duly	
dumb	er, est, ly, ness
dumm y	ies
dump	ed, ing, s
dumpling	s
dunce	s
dungarees	
dungeon	s
duplicate	d, ǿing, s
durable	ness
duration	
during	
dusk	
dusk y	ier, iest, ily, iness
dust	ed, ing, man, men, bin, pan, er, s
dust y	ier, iest, ily, iness
dutiful	ly, ness
dut y	ies

dw

dwarf	ed, ing, s or **dwarves**
dwell	ed, ing, er, s
dwelling	-house, -place, s
dwelt or **dwelled**	
dwindle	d, ǿing, s

dy

dye* (colour)	r, s
dyed* (coloured)	
dyeing* (colouring)	
dying* (losing life)	
dyke or **dike**	s
dynamic	al, ally, s
dynamite	d, ǿing, s
dynamo	s

ǿ Drop **e** before adding *ing*

*	due	dual		dye	dyed	dyeing
	dew	duel		die	died	dying
	Jew	jewel				

ea

each	
eager	*ly, ness*
eagle	*t, s*
ear	*ache, -drum, phone, -plug, -ring, s*
earwig	*s*
earl	*dom, s*
earl *y*	*ier, iest, iness*
earn* (be paid)	*ed, ing, er, s*
earnt or **earned**	
earnest	*ly, ness*
earth	*quake, worm, work, s*
earthen	*ware*
ease	*d, ∅ing, s*
eas *y*	*ier, iest, ily, iness*
easel	*s*
east	*ern, erly, ward, wards*
Easter	*-egg, s*
eat	*able, en, ing, er s*
eavesdrop	*ped, ping, per, s*

ec

eccentric	*s*
echo	*ed, ing, es*
éclair	*s*
eclipse	*d, ∅ing, s*
economic	*al, ally, s*
economize	*d, ∅ing, s*
econom *y*	*ies*

ed

eddy	*ing*
edd *ied*	*ies*
edge	*d, ∅ing, ways, wise, s*
edible	

edit	*ed, ing, s*
edition	*s*
editor	*ial, s*
educate	*d, ∅ing, s*
education	*al, ally, alist, ist*

ee

eel	*s*
eer *ie* or **eer** *y*	*ier, iest, ily, iness*

ef

effect	*ed, ing, s*
effective	*ly, ness*
efficiency	
efficient	*ly*
effig *y*	*ies*
effort	*less, lessly, s*

eg

egg	*-cup, -shell, -spoon, -timer, s*

ei

eiderdown	*s*
either	

el

elaborate	*d, ∅ing, ly, ness, s*
elapse	*d, ∅ing, s*
elastic	*ally, ity*
elbow	*ed, ing, s*
elder	*ly, s*
eldest	
elect	*ed, ing, ion, or, s*

*∅ Drop **e** before adding ing*

* earn
urn

em   en

electric	al, ally, s
electrician	s
electricity	
electrocute	d, ei̸ng, s
elegant	ly
elephant	s
elevator	s
elf	in, ish, **elves**
eligible	
eliminate	d, ei̸ng, s
elimination	s
Elizabethan	s
elm	-tree, s
elocution	ist
elope	d, ei̸ng, ment, s
else	where

em

embankment	s
embark	ed, ing, ation, s
embarrass	ed, ing, es
embarrassment	s
emblem	s
embrace	d, ei̸ng, s
embroider	ed, ing, s
embroider y	ies
emerald	s
emerge	d, ei̸ng, s
emergenc y	ies
emigrate	d, ei̸ng, s
emperor	s
empire	s
employ	ed, ing, ment, ee, er, s
empress	es
empty	ing
empt ied	ier, iest, ily, iness, ies

en

enable	d, ei̸ng, s
enamel	led, ling, s
encamp	ed, ing, ment, s
enchant	ed, ing, ment, s
encircle	d, ei̸ng, ment, s
enclose	d, ei̸ng, s
enclosure	s
encore	d, ei̸ng, s
encounter	ed, ing, s
encourage	d, ei̸ng, ment, s
encyclop(a)edia	s
end	ed, ing, less, lessly, s
endanger	ed, ing, s
endeavour	ed, ing, s
endure	d, ei̸ng, s
endurance	s
enem y	ies
energetic	ally
energ y	ies
enforce	d, ei̸ng, ment, s
engage	d, ei̸ng, ment, s
engine	-driver, -room, s
engineer	ed, ing, s
engrave	d, ei̸ng, r, s
engulf	ed, ing, s
enjoy	able, ed, ing, ment, s
enlarge	d, ei̸ng, r, ment, s
enlist	ed, ing, ment, s
enormous	ly, ness
enough	
enquire or **inquire**	d, ei̸ng, r, s
enquir y or **inquir** y	ies
enrage	d, ei̸ng, s
enrol	led, ling, ment, s
entangle	d, ei̸ng, ment, s
enter	ed, ing, s

ei̸ Drop **e** before adding *ing*

ep eq er   es ev

enterprise	*s*
entertain	*ed, ing, ment, er, s*
enthusiasm	*s*
enthusiastic	*ally*
entire	*ly, ness*
entitle	*d, ẹing, ment, s*
entrance	*s*
entry	*ies*
envelope	*s*
envious	*ly, ness*
environment	*al, alist, s*
envy	*ing*
envied	*ies*

ep

epidemic	*s*
epilogue	*s*
episode	*s*

eq

equal	*led, ling, ly, s*
equalize	*d, ẹing, r, s*
equator	*ial*
equip	*ped, ping, ment, s*
equivalent	*ly*

er

erase	*d, ẹing, r, s*
erect	*ed, ing, ion, s*
err	*ed, ing, ant, s*
errand	*s*
erratic	*ally*
error	*s*
erupt	*ed, ing, ion, s*

es

escalator	*s*
escapade	*s*
escape	*d, ẹing, r, s*
escort	*ed, ing, s*
Eskimo	*s or es or* **Eskimo**
especial	*ly*
espionage	
esplanade	*s*
essay	*ist, s*
essence	*s*
essential	*ly, s*
establish	*ed, ing, es*
establishment	*s*
estate	*s*
estimate	*d, ẹing, s*
estuary	*ies*

ev

evacuate	*d, ẹing, s*
evacuation	*s*
evade	*d, ẹing, s*
evaporate	*d, ẹing, s*
eve	*s*
even	*ed, ing, ly, ness, s*
evening	*s*
event	*ful, less, s*
eventual	*ly*
ever	*green, lasting, more*
every	*body, one, thing, where*
evict	*ed, ing, ion, s*
evidence	*s*
evident	*ly*
evil	*ly, ness, s*
evolve	*d, ẹing, s*
evolution	*s*

*ẹ Drop **e** before adding ing*

ex

ex

exact	ly, ness
exaggerate	d, ȩing, s
examination	s
examine	d, ȩing, r, s
examiner	s
example	s
exasperate	d, ȩing, s
excavate	d, ȩing, s
excavation	s
exceed	ed, ing, ingly, s
excel	led, ling, s
excellent	ly
except* (leaving out)	ed, ing, s
exception	al, ally, s
excess	ive, ively, es
exchange	d, ȩing, able, s
excitable	
excite	d, dly, ȩing, ment, s
exclaim	ed, ing, s
exclude	d, ȩing, s
exclusive	ly, ness
excursion	s
excuse	d, ȩing, s
execute	d, ȩing, s
execution	er, s
exercise	d, ȩing, s
exert	ed, ing, ion, s
exhaust	ed, ing, ion, ible, ive, -pipe, s
exhibit	ed, ing, or, s
exhibition	s
exile	d, ȩing, s
exist	ed, ing, ence, ent, s
exit	s
expand	ed, ing, s
expanse	s
expansion	s

expect	ed, ing, ant, ation, s
expedition	s
expel	led, ling, s
expense	s
expensive	ly, ness
experience	d, ȩing, s
experiment	ed, ing, al, ally, s
expert	ise, ly, ness, s
expire	d, ȩing, s
explain	ed, ing, s
explanation	s
explode	d, ȩing, s
exploit	s
exploration	s
explore	d, ȩing, r, s
explosion	s
explosive	s
export	ed, ing, er, s
expose	d, ȩing, s
exposure	s
express	ed, ing, es
expression	s
exquisite	ly, ness
extend	ed, ing, s
extension	s
extensive	ly, ness
extent	
exterior	s
extinct	ion
extinguish	ed, ing, es
extra	s
extract	ed, ing, ion, s
extraordinary	ily, iness
extravagance	s
extravagant	ly
extreme	ly, s
extricate	d, ȩing, s

ȩ Drop **e** before adding *ing*

* except
　accept

ey fa   fe

ey

eye *d, ball, brow, lid, sight, sore, s*
eyeing or **eying**
eyelash   *es*

fa

fable   *s*
fabulous   *ly, ness*
face *d, ǿing, -cloth, -flannel, s*
fact   *s*
factor *y*   *ies*
fade   *d, ǿing, s*
faggot   *s*
fail   *ed, ing, ure, s*
faint *er, est, ish, ly, ness, ed, ing, s*
fair* *er, est, ish, ly, ness, ground, s*
fair *y*   *ies*
faith   *s*
faithful   *ly, ness*
fake   *d, ǿing, s*
falcon   *er, s*
fall   *en, ing, s*
false   *hood, r, st, ly, ness*
falter   *ed, ing, s*
fame   *d*
familiar   *ity, ly*
famil *y*   *ies*
famine   *s*
famish   *ed, ing, es*
famous   *ly*
fan *ned, ning, ner, -belt, light, tail, s*
fancy   *ing*
fanc *ied ier, iest, ies, iful, ifully*
fantastic   *ally*
far *ther,* *thest, -away, -off, -fetched*
fare* (price of journey; food) *s*

fe

farewell   *s*
farm *ed, ing, er, -house, yard, s*
fascinate   *d, ǿing, s*
fashion *able, ably, ed, ing, s*
fast   *er, est, ness, ed, ing, s*
fasten   *ed, ing, er, s*
fat   *ted, ter, test, ness, s*
fatten   *ed, ing, s*
fatt *y*   *ier, iest, iness*
fatal   *ly*
fate* (destiny)   *d, ful, s*
father* (parent)   *less, ly, s*
fathom   *ed, ing, s*
fatigue   *d, ǿing, s*
fault *ed, ing, less, lessly, s*
fault *y*   *ier, iest, ily, iness*
favour *able, ably, ed, ing, itism, s*
favourite   *s*
fawn   *ed, ing, s*

fe

fear   *ed, ing, some, s*
fearful   *ly, ness*
fearless   *ly, ness*
feast   *ed, ing, s*
feat* (difficult deed)   *s*
feather *ed, ing, y, -bed, -duster, s*
feature   *d, ǿing, s*
February   *s*
fed
fee   *s*
feeble   *r, st, ness*
feebly
feed   *ing, er, s*
feel   *ing, er, s*
feet* (pl. of foot)

*ǿ Drop **e** before adding ing*

*	fair	farther	fate	feat
	fare	father	fête	feet

fi

feign	ed, ing, s
fell	ed, ing, s
fellow	ship, s
felt	
female	s
feminine	s
fence	d, ∅ing, r, s
fend	ed, ing, er, s
fern	s
ferocious	ly, ness
ferocity	
ferret	ed, ing, er, s
ferry	-boat, ing, man, men
ferried	ies
fertile	ly
fertilize	d, ∅ing, r, s
fester	ed, ing, s
festival	s
festive	ly
festivity	ies
fetch	ed, ing, es
fête* (entertainment; festival)	d, ∅ing, s
feud	s
feudal	ism
fever	ish, ishly, s
few	er, est

fi

fiancé* (masc.)	s
fiancée* (fem.)	s
fibre	glass, -tip, s
fiction	al
fictitious	ly, ness
fiddle	d, ∅ing, r, stick, s
fidget	ed, ing, y, s
field	ed, ing, sman, smen, er, s

fiend	ish, s
fierce	r, st, ly, ness
fiery	ier, iest, ily, iness
fight	ing, er, s
figure	d, ∅ing, s
file	d, ∅ing, s
fill	ed, ing, er, s
fillet	ed, ing, s
film	ed, ing, -set, -star, -studio, s
filter	ed, ing, -bed, -paper, -tip, s
filth	
filthy	ier, iest, ily, iness
final	ly, ist, s
finch	es
find* (found)	ing, er, s
fine	d,* ∅ing, s
fine	r, st, ly, ness
finger	ed, ing, -mark, -nail, -print, tip, s
finish	ed, ing, es
fiord or **fjord**	s
fir*	-cone, -tree, s
fire	d, ∅ing, man, men, place, work, s
fire	-alarm, -brigade, -engine, -escape, s
fire	-drill, -extinguisher, side, -station, s
firm	er, est, ly, ness, s
first	ly, -aid, -class, -floor, hand, -rate, s
fish	ed, ing, -meal, -paste, y, es or **fish**
fisher	man, men, s
fishing	-boat, -line, -net, -rod, -tackle
fishmonger	s
fist	s
fit	ted, ting, ter, test, ful, ly, ness, ment, s
fix	ed, ing, es
fixture	s
fizz	ed, ing, es
fizzy	ier, iest, ily, iness
fizzle	d, ∅ing, s

∅ Drop **e** before adding *ing*

*	fête	fiancé	find	fir
	fate	fiancée	fined	fur

fl_a   fle   fli   flo   flu   fly

fl	
flag	ged, ging, -day, -pole, -staff, s
flagon	s
flake	d, ∉ing, s
flame	d, ∉ing, -thrower, s
flamingo	es or s
flan	s
flank	ed, ing, s
flannel	s
flap	ped, ping, per, jack, s
flare	d, ∉ing, s
flash	ed, ing, es
flash y	ier, iest, ily, iness
flask	s
flat	ter, test, ly, ness, let, s
flatten	ed, ing, s
flatter	ed, ing, y, er, s
flavour	ed, ing, less, s
flaw	ed, less, s
flea* (insect)	-bite, -bitten, s
fleck	ed, ing, s
fledg(e)ling	s
fled	
flee* (run away)	ing, s
fleece	d, ∉ing, s
fleec y	ier, iest, ily, iness
fleet	ing, er, est, ly, ness, s
flesh	-coloured, -wound
flew* (fly)	
flex	ible, ibility, ed, ing, es
flick	ed, ing, s
flicker	ed, ing, s
flier or **flyer**	s
flight	-deck, -recorder, -test, s
flims y	ier, iest, ily, iness
flinch	ed, ing, es
fling	ing, s

flint	lock, stone, s
flint y	ier, iest, ily, iness
flip	ped, ping, per, s
flirt	ed, ing, ation, s
flit	ted, ting, s
float	ed, ing, er, s
flock	ed, ing, s
flog	ged, ging, s
flood	ed, ing, gate, lit, -lighting, -light, s
floor	ed, ing, -board, -cloth, -show, s
flop	ped, ping, s
flopp y	ier, iest, ily, iness
floral	ly
florist	s
flounder	ed, ing, s
flour* (ground wheat)	ed, ing, y, s
flourish	ed, ing, es
flow	ed, ing, s
flower*	ed, ing, y, -bed, -garden, -pot, s
flown	
flu* (influenza)	
flue* (chimney-pipe)	-pipe, s
fluent	ly
fluff	ed, ing, s
fluff y	ier, iest, ily, iness
fluid	s
fluke	d, ∉ing, s
flung	
flurry	ing
flurr ied	ies
flush	ed, ing, es
fluster	ed, ing, s
flute	-player, s
flutter	ed, ing, s
fl y	ies
flyer or **flier**	s
flying	-fish, -machine, -saucer, -squad

∉ Drop **e** before adding *ing*

* flea   flew   flour
   flee   flue   flower
          flu

fo

fo	
foal	*ed, ing, s*
foam	*ed, ing, -rubber, s*
foam *y*	*ier, iest, iness*
fo'c'sle or **forecastle**	*s*
focus	*ed, ing, es* or **foci**
foe	*s*
fog	*ged, ging, -horn, -lamp, -signal, s*
fogg *y*	*ier, iest, ily, iness*
foil	*ed, ing, s*
fold	*ed, ing, er, s*
foliage	
folk	*-dance, lore, -song, -tale, s* or **folk**
follow	*ed, ing, er, s*
foll *y*	*ies*
fond	*er, est, ly, ness*
fondle	*d, ∉ing, s*
food	*stuff, store, s*
fool	*ed, ing, hardy, s*
foolish	*ly, ness*
foot	*ing, hold, path, sore, work,* **feet**
football	*er, s*
footprint	*s*
footstep	*s*
for*	
forbad or **forbade**	
forbid	*den, ding, s*
force	*d, ∉ing, s*
ford	*ed, ing, s*
fore* (front)	*arm, ground, most, man, men*
forecast	*ing, er, s*
forehead	*s*
foreign	
foreigner	*s*
forest	*ry, er, s*
foretell	*ing, er, s*
foretold	

forever	*more*
forfeit	*ed, ing, ure, s*
forgave	
forge	*d, ∉ing, r, s*
forger *y*	*ies*
forget	*ting, -me-not, s*
forgetful	*ly, ness*
forgot	*ten*
forgive	*n, ∉ing, ness, s*
fork	*ed, ing, s*
forlorn	*ly, ness*
form	*ed, ing, ation, s*
former	*ly*
formidable	
formula	*e* or *s*
fort* (castle)	*s*
forth* (forward)	*coming*
fortification	*.s*
fortify	*ing*
fortif *ied*	*ies*
fortnight	*ly*
fortress	*es*
fortunate	*ly*
fortune	*-teller, s*
forward	*ed, ing, ly, 'ness, s*
fossil	*s*
fought* (fight)	
foul* (dirty)	*ed, ing, er, est, ly, ness, s*
found	*ed, ing, er*
foundation	*-stone, s*
foundr *y*	*ies*
fountain	*-pen, s*
fowl* (bird)	*s* or **fowl**
fox	*es, hounds, hunting, y*
foxglove	*s*
fox-terrier	*s*
foyer	*s*

∉ Drop **e** *before adding* ing

*	for	fort	forth	foul
	fore	fought	fourth (4th)	fowl
	four (4)			

fr

fraction	s
fracture	d, ɇing, s
fragile	ly, ness
fragment	s
fragrance	s
fragrant	ly
frail	er, est, ly, ty, ness
frame	d, ɇing, r, work, s
franc* (foreign coin)	s
frank* (candid, etc.)	er, est, ly, ness, s
frankincense	
frantic	ally, ly
fraud	s
fray	ed, ing, s
freak	ish, s
freckle	d, ɇing, s
free	d, ing, r, st, ly, dom, -style, way, s
freeze* (ice; cold)	r, s
freezing	-point
freight	er, s
frequent	ly, ed, ing, s
fresh	er, est, ly, ness
freshen	ed, ing, er, s
fret	ted, ting, ful, fully, s
fret	work, saw, s
friar	s
Friday	s
fried	
friend	ship, s
friendly	ier, iest, iness
frieze* (wall decoration)	s
frigate	s
fright	s
frighten	ed, ing, s
frightful	ly, ness
frill	ed, ing, y, s

fringe	d, ɇing, s
frisk	ed, ing, s
frisky	ier, iest, ily, iness
fritter	ed, ing, s
frivolous	ly, ness
frizz	ed, ing, es
frizzy	ier, iest, ily, iness
frock	s
frog	-spawn, s
frolic	ked, king, some, s
front	ed, ing, s
frontier	s
frost	ed, ing, -bite, -bitten, s
frosty	ier, iest, ily, iness
froth	ed, ing, s
frothy	ier, iest, ily, iness
frown	ed, ing, s
froze	n
frugal	ity, ly
fruit	-cake, -juice, -tree, s
fry	er, ing
fried	ies

fu

fudge	
fuel	led, ling, s
fugitive	s
fulfil	led, ling, ment, s
full	er, est, y, ness
fumble	d, ɇing, r, s
fume	d, ɇing, s
fun	fair
funny	ier, iest, ily, iness
function	ed, ing, s
fund	s
funeral	s

ɇ Drop e before adding ing

ga

fungus	*es* or **fungi**
funnel	*led, ling, s*
fur* (animal's coat)	*rier, s*
furr *y*	*ier, iest, ily, iness*
furious	*ly, ness*
furl	*ed, ing, s*
furnace	*s*
furnish	*ed, ing, ings, es*
furniture	
furrow	*ed, ing, s*
further	*ed, ing, more, most, s*
furthest	
furtive	*ly, ness*
fur *y*	*ies*
furze	*s*
fuse	*d, ǿing, s*
fuselage	*s*
fuss	*ed, ing, es*
fuss *y*	*ier, iest, ily, iness*
futile	*ly*
future	*s*
fuzz *y*	*ier, iest, ily, iness*

ga

gabardine or **gaberdine**	
gabble	*d, ǿing, r, s*
gag	*ged, ging, s*
gaiet *y*	*ies*
gaily	
gain	*ed, ing, s*
gait* (way of walking)	*s*
gala	*s*
galactic	
galax *y*	*ies*
gale	*s*
gallant	*ly, s*

galleon	*s*
galler *y*	*ies*
galley	*-slave, s*
gallon	*s*
gallop	*ed, ing, s*
gallows	
gamble* (bet)	*d, ǿing, r, s*
gambol* (leap; frisk)	*led, ling, s*
game	*r, st, ly, ness, keeper, s*
gander	*s*
gang	*ed, ing, ster, s*
gangway	*s*
gaol or **jail**	*ed, ing, er, s*
gape	*d, ǿing, r, s*
garage	*d, ǿing, s*
garbage	
garden	*ed, ing, er, s*
gargle	*d, ǿing, s*
garland	*ed, ing, s*
garlic	
garment	*s*
garret	*s*
garrison	*ed, ing, s*
garter	*s*
gas	*sed, sing, es*
gash	*ed, ing, es*
gasp	*ed, ing, s*
gate* (door)	*keeper, post, way, s*
gather	*ed, ing, er, s*
gaud *y*	*ier, iest, ily, iness*
gauge	*d, ǿing, s*
gauntlet	*s*
gauze	*s*
gave	
gay	*er, est*
gaily	
gaze	*d, ǿing, r, s*

ǿ Drop **e** before adding *ing*

*	fur	gait	gamble
	fir	gate	gambol

ge

gear	*ed, ing, case, -lever, wheel, s*
geese	
Geiger counter	*s*
gem	*s*
general	*s*
generally	
generate	*d, ǿing, s*
generation	*s*
generator	*s*
generosity	
generous	*ly*
genie	**genii**
genius	*es*
gentle	*r, st, ness, man, men*
gently	
genuine	*ly, ness*
geograph *y*	*ical, ically*
geologist	*s*
geolog *y*	*ical, ically*
geometr *y*	*ic, ical, ically*
Georgian	*s*
geranium	*s*
germ	*s*
germinate	*d, ǿing, s*
germination	*s*
gesticulate	*d, ǿing, s*
gesture	*d, ǿing, s*
get	*ting, ter, away, s*
geyser	*s*

gh

ghastl *y*	*ier, iest, ily, iness*
gherkin	*s*
ghost	*s*
ghostl *y*	*ier, iest, ily, iness*

gi

giant	*-killer, s*
gidd *y*	*ier, iest, ily, iness*
gift	*ed, s*
gigantic	*ally*
giggle	*d, ǿing, r, s*
gild* (cover with gold)	*ed, ing, er, s*
gilt* (gold covering)	
ginger	*-ale, -beer, bread, -snap, s*
gips *y* or **gyps** *y*	*ies*
giraffe	*s*
girder	*s*
girl	*ish, -friend, s*
Girl Guide	*s*
give	*n, ǿing, r, s*

gl

glacier	*s*
glad	*der, dest, ly, ness*
gladden	*ed, ing, s*
glade	*s*
gladiator	*s*
gladiolus	*es* or **gladioli**
glamour	
glamorous	*ly*
glance	*d, ǿing, s*
glare	*d, ǿing, s*
glass	*es*
gleam	*ed, ing, s*
glean	*ed, ing, er, s*
glee	*ful, fully*
glide	*d, ǿing, r, s*
glimmer	*ed, ing, s*
glimpse	*d, ǿing, s*
glint	*ed, ing, s*
glisten	*ed, ing, s*

ǿ Drop **e** before adding *ing*

*	gild	gilt	
	guild	guilt	

gn go   gra

glitter	*ed, ing, s*
gloat	*ed, ing, s*
globe	*-trotter, s*
glockenspiel	*s*
gloom	
gloom *y*	*ier, iest, ily, iness*
glor *y*	*ied, ies*
glorious	*ly*
gloss *y*	*ier, iest, ily, iness*
glove	*-puppet, s*
glow	*ed, ing, -worm, s*
glue	*d, ǿing, y, -pot, s*
glum	*mer, mest, ly, ness*

gn

gnash	*ed, ing, es*
gnat	*-bite, s*
gnaw	*n, ed, ing, er, s*
gnome	*s*

go

goal	*keeper, -kick, -mouth, -post, s*
goat	*herd, skin, s*
gobble	*d, ǿing, r, s*
goblet	*s*
goblin	*s*
god	*son, father, mother, parent, s*
goddess	*es*
godchild	*ren*
goes	
going	*s*
goggle	*d, ǿing, s*
gold	*en, -dust, -field, -mine, -smith*
goldfish	*es or* **goldfish**
golf	*ing, -club, -course, -links, er, s*

golliwog	*s*
gondola	*s*
gondolier	*s*
gone	
gong	*s*
good	*-hearted, ly, ness, s*
good-bye	*s*
goose	**geese**
gooseberr *y*	*ies*
gore	*d, ǿing, s*
gorge	*d, ǿing, s*
gorgeous	*ly, ness*
gorilla	*s*
gorse	*s*
gosling	*s*
gossip	*ed, ing, er, s*
govern	*ed, ing, or, ment, s*
governess	*es*
gown	*s*

gr

grab	*bed, bing, ber, s*
grace	*d, ǿing, s*
graceful	*ly, ness*
gracious	*ly, ness*
grade	*d, ǿing, s*
gradient	*s*
gradual	*ly, ness*
grain	*s*
grammar	
gramophone	*s*
grand	*er, est, ly, ness, stand*
grand	*father, pa, mother, ma, parents*
grandad or **grand-dad**	*s*
grandchild	*ren*
grann *y*	*ies*

ǿ Drop **e** *before adding* ing

grange	*s*	**grill*** (cook)	*ed, ing, er, s*
granite		**grille*** (grating)	*s*
grant	*ed, ing, s*	**grim**	*mer, mest, ly, ness*
grape	*fruit, -vine, s*	**grime**	
graph	*ed, ing, s*	**grim** *y*	*ier, iest, ily, iness*
grapple	*d, ∉ing, s*	**grin**	*ned, ning, ner, s*
grasp	*ed, ing, s*	**grind**	*ing, er, stone, s*
grass	*ed, ing, es*	**grip**	*ped, ping, per, s*
grass *y*	*ier, iest, iness*	**gristle**	
grasshopper	*s*	**grit**	*ted, ting, ter, s*
grass-snake	*s*	**gritt** *y*	*ier, iest, ily, iness*
grate* (fireplace; rub)	*r,* d, ∉ing, s*	**grizzle**	*d, ∉ing, r, s*
grateful	*ly, ness*	**groan*** (moan)	*ed, ing, er, s*
grating	*s*	**grocer**	*s*
gratitude		**grocer** *y*	*ies*
grave	*r, st, ly, ness*	**groom**	*ed, ing, s*
grave	*-digger, stone, yard, s*	**groove**	*d, ∉ing, s*
gravel	*led, ling, ly, -path, -pit, s*	**grope**	*d, ∉ing, s*
gravit *y*	*ies*	**grotesque**	*ly, ness*
grav *y*	*ies*	**grotto**	*es or s*
graze	*d, ∉ing, s*	**ground**	*ed, ing, sheet, sman, smen, s*
grease	*d, ∉ing, r, -paint, -proof, s*	**group**	*ed, ing, -leader, s*
greas *y*	*ier, iest, ily, iness*	**grove**	*s*
great* (large)	*er,* est, ly, ness, s*	**grovel**	*led, ling, ler, s*
greed		**grow**	*th, ing, er, s*
greed *y*	*ier, iest, ily, iness*	**grown*** (got bigger)	
green	*er, est, ly, ness, ery, ish, y, s*	**grown-up**	*s*
greengrocer	*s*	**growl**	*ed, ing, er, s*
greenhouse	*s*	**grub**	*bed, bing, ber, s*
greet	*ed, ing, s*	**grubb** *y*	*ier, iest, ily, iness*
grenade	*s*	**grudge**	*d, ∉ing, s*
grenadier	*s*	**gruel**	
grew		**gruesome**	*ly, ness*
grey	*er, est, ly, ness, ish, hound, s*	**gruff**	*er, est, ly, ness*
grief	*-stricken, s*	**grumble**	*d, ∉ing, r, s*
grievance	*s*	**grump** *y*	*ier, iest, ily, iness*
grieve	*d, ∉ing, s*	**grunt**	*ed, ing, er, s*

*∉ Drop **e** before adding ing*

*	grate	grater	grill	groan
	great	greater	grille	grown

gu gy   ha

gu	**ha**

guarantee	*d, ing, s*	**habit**	*s*
guard	*ed, ing, sman, smen, room, s*	**hack**	*ed, ing, er, s*
guardian	*s*	**haddock**	*s* or **haddock**
guess	*ed,* ing, es, work*	**hadn't** (had not)	
guest* (visitor)	*-night, -house, -room, s*	**hail**	*ed, ing, er, stone, storm, s*
guide	*d, e̸ing, -dog, -book, -post, s*	**hair***	*dresser, -dryer, pin, -slide, -style, s*
guild* (society)	*hall, s*	**hair** y	*ier, iest, iness*
guillotine	*d, e̸ing, s*	**hake**	*s* or **hake**
guilt* (wrongdoing)	*less, lessly*	**half**	*-price, -term, -time, -way,* **halves**
guilt y	*ier, iest, ily, iness*	**halfpenn** y	*ies* or **halfpence**
guinea-pig	*s*	**hall*** (room; passage)	*way, s*
guitar	*ist, s*	**hallo** or **hello** or **hullo**	*ed, ing, s*
gulf	*s*	**halo**	*es* or *s*
gull	*s*	**halt**	*ed, ing, s*
gull y	*ies*	**halve**	*d, e̸ing, s*
gulp	*ed, ing, s*	**hamburger**	*s*
gum	*med, ming, boil, -tree, s*	**hammer**	*ed, ing, s*
gumm y	*ier, iest, iness*	**hammock**	*s*
gun	*ned, ning, ner, nery, man, men, s*	**hamper**	*ed, ing, s*
gun	*fire, point, powder, shot, smith, s*	**hamster**	*s*
gurgle	*d, e̸ing, s*	**hand**	*ed, ing, bag, work, writing, ful, s*
gush	*ed, ing, es*	**handcuff**	*ed, ing, s*
gust	*ed, ing, s*	**handicap**	*ped, ping, per, s*
gust y	*ier, iest, ily, iness*	**handicraft**	
gut	*ted, ting, s*	**handiwork**	
gutter	*s*	**handkerchief**	*s*
guy	*s*	**handle**	*d, e̸ing, r, -bar, s*
guzzle	*d, e̸ing, r, s*	**handsome**	*r, st, ly, ness*
		hand y	*ier, iest, ily, iness*
		hang	*ed, ing, -gliding, -glider, s*
gy		**hangar*** (aeroplane shed)	*s*
gymkhana	*s*	**hanger*** (for clothes, etc.)	*s*
gymnasium	*s* or **gymnasia**	**happen**	*ed, ing, s*
gymnast	*ic, s*	**happ** y	*ier, iest, ily, iness*
gymslip	*s*	**harbour**	*ed, ing, -master, s*
gyps y or **gips** y	*ies*	**hard**	*er, est, ish, ly, ness, -hearted, ware*

*e̸ Drop **e** before adding ing*

harden	ed, ing, er, s
hardship	s
hare* (animal)	s
hark	en
harm	ed, ing, s
harmful	ly, ness
harmless	ly, ness
harness	ed, ing, es
harp	ist, s
harpoon	ed, ing, -gun, s
harsh	er, est, ly, ness
hart* (stag)	s
harvest	ed, ing, er, s
hasn't (has not)	
haste	d, ∉ing, s
hasten	ed, ing, s
hasty	ier, iest, ily, iness
hat	band, -peg, -pin, stand, -trick, ful, s
hatch	ed, ing, es
hatchet	s
hate	d, ∉ing, r, s
hateful	ly, ness
hatred	
haughty	ier, iest, ily, iness
haul* (pull)	age, ed, ing, ier, s
haunt	ed, ing, s
have	∉ing
haven't (have not)	
haversack	s
havoc	
haw	thorn, s
hawk	ed, ing, er, s
hay	field, maker, making, rick, stack, s
hazard	ed, ing, ous, ously, s
hazel	nut, -tree, s
haze	s
hazy	ier, iest, ily, iness

he

head	ed, ing, ache, long, light, way, s
headmaster	s
headmistress	es
headquarters	
heal* (cure)	ed, ing, er, s
health	
healthy	ier, iest, ily, iness
heap	ed, ing, s
hear* (listen)	ing, s
heard* (listened)	
heart* (of body)	ache, -broken, less, s
hearten	ed, ing, s
hearty	ier, iest, ily, iness
hearth	-rug, s
heat	ed, edly, ing, er, -stroke, wave, s
heath	land, s
heathen	s
heather	s
heave	d, ∉ing, r, s
heaven	ly, ward, s
heavy	ier, iest, ily, iness
he'd (he had; he would)	
hedge	d, ∉ing, hog, row, -sparrow, s
heed	ed, ing, ful, less, s
heel* (back of foot)	ed, ing, s
hefty	ier, iest, ily, iness
heifer	s
height	s
heighten	ed, ing, s
heir* (one who inherits)	loom, s
heiress	es
held	
helicopter	s
he'll (he will; he shall)	
hello or **hallo** or **hullo**	ed, ing, s
helm	sman, smen, s

∉ Drop **e** before adding *ing*

*	hare	haul	hart	heal	hear	heard	heir
	hair	hall	heart	heel	here	herd	air

hi   ho

helmet	s
help	ed, ing, er, s
helpful	ly, ness
helpless	ly, ness
helter-skelter	s
hem	med, ming, -line, s
her	self, s
herald	ed, ing, s
herb	age, al, alist, s
herd* (of cattle, etc.)	ed, ing, sman, s
here* (in this place)	about(s), by, with
here's (here is)	
hermit	age, -crab, s
hero	es
heroic	al, ally, s
heroine	s
heroism	
heron	s
herring	-gull, s or **herring**
he's (he is; he has)	
hesitate	d, ¢ing, s
hesitation	s
hew* (chop; cut)	n, ed, ing, er, s
hexagon	al, s

hi

hibernate	d, ¢ing, s
hibernation	
hiccup	ed, ing, s
hid	den
hide	¢ing, -and-seek, away, -out, s
hideous	ly, ness
high	er*, est, ly, chair, light, -road, s
highland	er, s
Highness	es
highway	man, men, s

hijack	ed, ing, er, s
hike	d, ¢ing, r, s
hilarious	ly, ness
hill	ock, side, top, s
hill y	ier, iest, iness
him* (he)	self
hinder	ed, ing, s
hindrance	s
hinge	d, ¢ing, s
hint	ed, ing, s
hippopotamus	es or **hippopotami**
hire* (rent)	d, ¢ing, -purchase, r, s
hiss	ed, ing, es
historic	al, ally
histor y	ies
hit	ting, ter, s
hitch	ed, ing, es
hitch-hike	d, ¢ing, r, s
hive	s

ho

hoard* (hidden store)	ed, ing, s
hoarse* (husky)	r, st, ly, ness
hobble	d, ¢ing, s
hobb y	ies
hockey	-stick
hoe	d, ing, s
hog	skin, s
hoist	ed, ing, s
hold	ing, -all, -up, er, s
hole* (hollow place)	d, ¢ing, s
holiday	ed, ing, -camp, -maker, s
hollow	ed, ing, ly, ness, s
holl y	ies
hollyhock	s
holster	s

¢ Drop **e** before adding *ing*

herd	here	hew	higher	him	hoard	hoarse	hole
heard	hear	hue	hire	hymn	horde	horse	whole

holy* (godly)	*ier, iest, ily, iness, ies*
home	*-grown, -made, work, ward, s*
homeless	*ness*
homely	*ier, iest, iness*
homesick	*ness*
honest	*ly, y*
honey	*-bee, dew, -pot, comb, suckle, s*
honeymoon	*ed, ing, er, s*
honour	*able, ably, ed, ing, s*
hood	*ed, ing, s*
hoof	*beat, mark, s* or **hooves**
hook	*ed, ing, er, s*
hooligan	*ism, s*
hoop	*ed, ing, -la, s*
hoot	*ed, ing, er, s*
hop	*ped, ping, per, s*
hope	*d, ∮ing, s*
hopeful	*ly, ness*
hopeless	*ly, ness*
horde* (crowd)	*s*
horizon	*tal, tally, s*
horn	*s*
hornpipe	*s*
hornet	*s*
horoscope	*s*
horrible	*ness*
horribly	
horrid	*ly, ness*
horrify	*ing*
horrified	*ies*
horror	*-stricken, -struck, s*
horse* (animal)	*back, man, men, shoe, s*
horse-chestnut	*-tree, s*
hose	*d, ∮ing, -pipe, s*
hospital	*s*
hospitality	
host	*s*

hostage	*s*
hostel	*led, ling, ler, s*
hostess	*es*
hostile	*ly*
hot	*ter, test, ly, ness, house, -plate*
hotel	*ier, s*
hound	*ed, ing, s*
hour* (sixty mins.)	*ly, -hand, s*
house	*d, ∮ing, hold, work, keeper, s*
housemaster	*s*
housemistress	*es*
housewife	*wives*
hover	*ed, ing, port, s, craft*
however	
howl	*ed, ing, er, s*

hu

huddle	*d, ∮ing, s*
hue* (colour)	*s*
hug	*ged, ging, s*
huge	*r, st, ly, ness*
hullo or **hallo** or **hello**	*ed, ing, s*
hum	*med, ming, mer, s*
human	*ity, ly*
humble	*d, ∮ing, r, st, ness, s*
humbly	
humid	*ity*
humiliate	*d, ∮ing, s*
humorous	*ly, ness*
humour	*ed, ing, s*
hump	*ed, ing, s*
hunch	*ed, ing, s*
hundred	*th, weight, s*
hung	
hunger	*ed, ing, s*
hungry	*ier, iest, ily, iness*

∮ Drop e before adding ing

*	holy	horde	horse		hour	hue
	wholly	hoard	hoarse		our	hew

hy ic   id ig il

hunt	*ed, ing, sman, smen, er, s*
hurdle	*d, ėing, r, s*
hurl	*ed, ing, er, s*
hurrah or **hurray**	*ed, ing, s*
hurricane	*-lamp, s*
hurry	*ing*
hurr *ied*	*iedly, ies*
hurt	*ing, s*
hurtle	*d, ėing, s*
husband	*s*
hush	*ed, ing, es*
husk *y*	*ier, iest, ily, iness*
hustle	*d, ėing, s*
hutch	*es*

hy

hyacinth	*s*
hydrangea	*s*
hydraulic	*ally, s*
hydrofoil	*s*
hydrogen	
hydroplane	*s*
hyena or **hyaena**	*s*
hygiene	
hygienic	*ally*
hymn* (song of praise)	*al, -book, s*
hypnotism	
hypnotist	*s*
hypnotize	*d, ėing, s*
hysteric	*al, ally, s*

ic

ice	*d, ėing, berg, -cream, -cube, s*
icicle	*s*
ic *y*	*ier, iest, ily, iness*

id

I'd (I would; I should; I had)	
idea	*s*
ideal	*ly, ism, ist, s*
identical	*ly*
identification	
identify	*ing*
identif *ied*	*ies*
identit *y*	*ies*
idiot	*s*
idiotic	*al, ally*
idle* (lazy)	*d, ėing, r, st, ness, s*
idly	
idol* (false god)	*s*
idolize	*d, ėing, s*

ig

igloo	*s*
ignite	*d, ėing, s*
ignorance	
ignorant	*ly*
ignore	*d, ėing, s*

il

I'll (I will)	
ill	*-bred, -mannered, -treated, s*
illness	*es*
illegal	*ly*
illegible	
illiterate	*ly, ness, s*
illuminate	*d, ėing, s*
illumination	*s*
illusion	*ist, s*
illustrate	*d, ėing, s*
illustration	*s*

ė Drop **e** before adding *ing*

*	hymn	idle
	him	idol

im   in

im		in	
I'm (I am)		**inaccurate**	ly
image	s	**inattentive**	ly, ness
imaginary		**incapable**	
imagination	s	**inch**	ed, ing, es
imagine	d, ∉ing, s	**incident**	al, ally, s
imitate	d, ∉ing, s	**incline**	d, ∉ing, s
imitation	s	**include**	d, ∉ing, s
immediate	ly, ness	**inclusive**	ly, ness
immense	ly, ness	**income**	s
immortal	ity, ly, s	**inconvenience**	d, ∉ing, s
immune		**inconvenient**	ly
immunize	d, ∉ing, s	**incorrect**	ly, ness
impatience		**increase**	d, ∉ing, s
impatient	ly	**incredibl**e	y
imperfect	ion, ly	**incurable**	ness, s
impersonate	d, ∉ing, s	**indeed**	
impersonation	s	**indefinite**	ly, ness
impertinence	s	**independent**	ly
impertinent	ly	**indicate**	d, ∉ing, s
implement	s	**indication**	s
implore	d, ∉ing, s	**indicator**	s
impolite	ly, ness	**indigestion**	
import	ed, ing, er, s	**indignant**	ly
importance		**indignation**	
important	ly	**indistinct**	ly, ness
impose	d, ∉ing, s	**individual**	ly, s
impossibility	ies	**indoor**	s
impossible		**industrial**	ly
impress	ed, ing, ive, es	**industrious**	ly
impression	able, s	**industr**y	ies
imprison	ed, ing, ment, s	**inexpensive**	ly, ness
improve	d, ∉ing, ment, s	**infant**	s
impudence		**infantry**	man, men
impudent	ly	**infect**	ed, ing, ious, ion, s
impure	ly	**inferior**	ity, ly, s
impurity	ies	**infirmar**y	ies

∉ Drop **e** before adding *ing*

inflammable	*ness*	**inspect**	*ed, ing, ion, or, s*
inflate	*d, ∉ing, s*	**inspiration**	*s*
influence	*d, ∉ing, s*	**inspire**	*d, ∉ing, s*
influenza		**install**	*ed, ing, ation, s*
inform	*ed, ing, ation, er, s*	**instalment**	*s*
infrequent	*ly*	**instance**	*s*
infuriate	*d, ∉ing, s*	**instant**	*aneous, ly*
ingredient	*s*	**instead**	
inhabit	*ed, ing, able, ant, s*	**instinct**	*ive, ively, s*
inhale	*d, ∉ing, s*	**institute**	*d, ∉ing, s*
inherit	*ed, ing, ance, s*	**institution**	*al, s*
initial	*led, ling, s*	**instruct**	*ed, ing, ive, ion, or, s*
inject	*ed, ing, ion, s*	**instrument**	*al, alist, s*
injure	*d, ∉ing, s*	**insufficient**	*ly*
injur *y*	*ies*	**insult**	*ed, ing, s*
ink *ed, ing, -bottle, -pot, stand, -well, s*		**insurance**	*s*
ink *y*	*ier, iest, iness*	**insure**	*d, ∉ing, s*
inland		**intact**	
inn	*keeper, s*	**intelligence**	
inner	*most*	**intelligent**	*ly*
innings		**intend**	*ed, ing, s*
innocence		**intense**	*ly, ness*
innocent	*ly, s*	**intent**	*ly, ness*
inoculate	*d, ∉ing, s*	**intention**	*al, ally, s*
inoculation	*s*	**intercept** *ed, ing, ive, ion, or s*	
inquire or **enquire** *d, ∉ing, r, s*		**interest**	*ed, ing, s*
inquir *y* or **enquir** *y*	*ies*	**interfere**	*d, ∉ing, nce, s*
inquisitive	*ly, ness*	**interior**	*s*
insane	*ly*	**interlude**	*s*
inscription	*s*	**intermediate**	*ly*
insect	*s*	**international**	*ly*
insensible		**interpret** *ed, ing, ation, er, s*	
insert	*ed, ing, ion, s*	**interrogate**	*d, ∉ing, s*
inside	*s*	**interrupt**	*ed, ing, ion, s*
insist	*ed, ing, ence, ent, s*	**interval**	*s*
insolence		**intervene**	*d, ∉ing, s*
insolent	*ly*	**interview**	*ed, ing, er, s*

*∉ Drop **e** before adding ing*

introduce	d, ꬵing, s
introduction	s
intrude	d, ꬵing, r, s
invade	d, ꬵing, r, s
invalid	ed, ing, s
invasion	s
invent	ed, ing, ive, ion, or, s
investigate	d, ꬵing, s
investigation	s
investigator	s
invisible	ness
invitation	s
invite	d, ꬵing, s
involve	d, ꬵing, s
inward	ly, s

ir

iris	es
iron	ed, ing, monger, work, s
ironing-board	s
irregular	ity, ly
irrigate	d, ꬵing, s
irrigation	s
irritabl e	y
irritabilit y	ies
irritate	d, ꬵing, s
irritation	s

is

island	er, s
isle* (island)	s
ısn't (is not)	
ısolate	d, ꬵing, s
isolation	
issue	d, ꬵing, s

it

italic	s
itch	ed, ing, es
itch y	ier, iest, iness
item	s
its* (belonging to it)	
it's* (it is)	
itself	

iv

I've (I have)	
ivor y	ies
iv y	ies

ja

jab	bed, bing, s
jabber	ed, ing, s
jack	ed, ing, pot, s
jackdaw	s
jacket	s
jade	d, ꬵing, s
jagged	ly, ness
jaguar	s
jail or gaol	ed, ing, er, s
jam	med, ming, my, -pot, -jar, s
jamboree	s
jangle	d, ꬵing, s
January	s
jar	red, ring, ful, s
jaunt	ed, ing, s
jaunt y	ier, iest, ily, iness
javelin	s
jaw	-bone, s
jay	s
jazz	ed, ing, y, es

ꬵ Drop **e** before adding *ing*

* isle / aisle   its / it's

je ji jo ju

je

jealous	*ly*
jealous *y*	*ies*
jeans	
jeep	*s*
jeer	*ed, ing, s*
jell *y*	*ied, ies*
jelly-fish	*es* or **jelly-fish**
jemm *y*	*ies*
jerk	*ed, ing, s*
jerk *y*	*ier, iest, ily, iness*
jerkin	*s*
jersey	*s*
jest	*ed, ing, er, s*
jet	*ted, ting, -liner, -plane, -fighter, s*
jettison	*ed, ing, s*
jett *y*	*ies*
Jew*	*ish, s*
jewel*	*led, ling, ler, -case, s*
jewellery or **jewelry**	

ji

jiff *y*	*ies*
jig	*ged, ging, ger, s*
jigsaw puzzle	*s*
jilt	*ed, ing, s*
jingle	*d, ∉ing, -jangle, s*
jiu-jitsu or **ju-jitsu** or **judo**	
jive	*d, ∉ing, s*

jo

job	*less, s*
jockey	*s*
jocular	*ity, ly*
jodhpurs	

ju

jog	*ged, ging, ger, s*
join	*ed, ing, ery, er, s*
joint	*ed, ing, ly, s*
joist	*s*
joke	*d, ∉ing, r, s*
jollit *y*	*ies*
joll *y*	*ier, iest, ily, iness*
jolt	*ed, ing, s*
jonquil	*s*
jostle	*d, ∉ing, s*
jot	*ted, ting, ter, s*
journal	*ism, ist, s*
journey	*ed, ing, s*
joust	*ed, ing, s*
jovial	*ity, ly*
joy	*s*
joyful	*ly, ness*
joyous	*ly, ness*

ju

jubilant	*ly*
jubilation	*s*
jubilee	*s*
judge	*d, ∉ing, s*
judg(e)ment	*s*
judo or **ju-jitsu** or **jiu-jitsu**	
juggle	*d, ∉ing, r, s*
juice	*s*
juic *y*	*ier, iest, ily, iness*
July	*s*
jumble	*d, ∉ing, -sale, s*
jump	*ed, ing, er, -jet, s*
jumper	*s*
jump *y*	*ier, iest, ily, iness*
junction	*s*
June	*s*

*∉ Drop **e** before adding *ing**

*	Jew	jewel
	dew	dual
	due	duel

jungle	s
junior	s
junk	-shop, s
junket	s
juror	s
jur y	ies
just	ly, ness
justice	
justify	ing
justif ied	ies
jut	ted, ting, s
juvenile	s

ka

kaleidoscope	s
kangaroo	s
karate	
kayak	s

ke

keel	ed, ing, s
keen	er, est, ly, ness
keep	ing, er, sake, s
kennel	-maid, s
kept	
kerb* (pavement edge)	side, stone, s
kernel* (nut; seed)	s
kestrel	s
ketchup	
kettle	-holder, ful, s
key*	hole, -ring, s

kh

khaki	s

ki

kick	ed, ing, -off, er, s
kid	skin, s
kidnap	ped, ping, per, s
kidney	-bean, s
kill	ed, ing, er, s
kiln	s
kilogram(me)	s
kilometre	s
kilt	s
kimono	s
kin	sfolk, sman, smen
kind	er, est, -hearted, s
kindl y	ier, iest, ily, iness
kindness	es
kindergarten	s
kindle	d, ɇing, s
king	dom, cup, fisher, s
kink	ed, ing, y, s
kiosk	s
kipper	s
kiss	ed, ing, es
kit	ted, ting, -bag, s
kitchen	ette, -maid, s
kite	s
kitten	s

kn

knack	s
knapsack	s
knave* (rogue)	s
knead* (work dough)	ed, ing, s
knee	-deep, -high, -cap, s
kneel	ed, ing, s
knelt or kneeled	
knew* (know)	

ɇ Drop **e** before adding *ing*

la

knife	d, ∉ing, -edge, -point, **knives**
knight* (Sir)	ed, ing, ly, -errant, hood, s
knit	ted, ting, ter, s
knitting-needle	s
knob	s
knobbl y	ier, iest, iness
knock	ed, ing, er, -out, s
knot* (tied string; sea speed)	ted, ting, s
knott y	ier, iest, ily, iness
know* (understand)	n, ing, ingly, s
knowledge	able
knuckle	d, ∉ing, -bone, -duster, s

la

label	led, ling, s
laborator y	ies
labour	ed, ing, er, s
lace	d, ∉ing, s
lack	ed, ing, s
lacquer	ed, ing, s
lacrosse	
ladder	ed, ing, s
laden	
lad y	ies
ladybird	s
lag	ged, ging, gard, s
lagoon	s
laid	
lain* (lie flat)	
lair* (den)	s
lake	s
lamb	ed, ing, -chop, kin, skin, swool, s
lame	d, ∉ing, r, st, ly, ness, s
lament	ed, ing, able, ation, s
lamp	light, -post, shade, -standard, s
lance	d, ∉ing, -corporal, r, s

land	ed, ing, mark, scape, slide, slip, s
landlad y	ies
landlord	s
lane* (narrow road)	s
language	s
lantern	s
lap	ped, ping, s
lapel	s
lapse	d, ∉ing, s
larch	es
lard	ed, ing, s
larder	s
large	r, st, ly, ness
lark	s
larva* (insect grub)	e
lash	ed, ing, es
lass	es
lasso	ed, ing, es or s
last	ed, ing, ly, s
latch	ed, ing, es
late	r, st, ly, ness
lathe	s
lather	ed, ing, s
latitude	s
latter	ly
laugh	able, ed, ing, s
laughter	
launch	ed, ing, es
launder	ette, ed, ing, s
laundress	es
laundr y	ies
laurel	s
lava* (volcanic rock)	s
lavator y	ies
lavender	-water
law	ful, less, -breaker, -court, s
lawyer	s

∉ Drop **e** before adding ing

knight	knot	know	lain	lair	larva
night	not	no	lane	layer	lava

le   li

lawn	-mower, -sprinkler, s
lay	ing, about, -by, out, er, s
laid	
layer* (coat; thickness)	ed, ing, s
laze	d, ∉ing, s
laz y	ier, iest, ily, iness

le

lead* (metal)	ed, en, -poisoning, s
lead (be first)	ing, er, s
leaf	ed, ing, less, -stalk, **leaves**
leaf y	ier, iest, iness
leaflet	s
league	s
leak* (hole; crack)	age, ed, ing, s
leak y	ier, iest, iness
lean	er, est, ly, ness
lean	ed, ing, s
leant* or **leaned**	
leap	ed, ing, frog, -year, s
leapt or **leaped**	
learn	ed, ing, er, s
learnt or **learned**	
least	
leather	y, s
leave	∉ing, r, s
lecture	d, ∉ing, r, s
led* (guided)	
ledge	s
leek* (vegetable)	s
left	
leg	ged, ging, less, -iron, -rest, s
legend	ary, s
legion	s
leisure	ly
lemon	ade, -drop, -juice, -peel, -tree, s

li

lend	ing, er, s
length	s
lengthen	ed, ing, s
length y	ier, iest, ily, iness
lenient	ly
lens	es
lent* (lend)	
leopard	skin, s
leotard	s
leper	s
leprosy	
less	er
lessen* (make smaller)	ed, ing, s
lesson* (thing learnt)	s
let	ting, s
let's (let us)	
letter	ed, ing, -writer, s
letter-box	es
lettuce	s
level	led, ling, -crossing, s
lever	age, ed, ing, s

li

liable	
liar* (one who lies)	s
liberal	s
libert y	ies
librarian	s
librar y	ies
licence* (noun)	s
license* (verb)	d, ∉ing, s
lick	ed, ing, er, s
licorice or **liquorice**	
lie	d, s
lying	
lieutenant	-colonel, -general, s

∉ Drop **e** before adding *ing*

*	layer	lead	leak	leant	lessen	liar	licence
	lair	led	leek	lent	lesson	lyre	license

lo

life	*less, like, line, long, size, time.* **lives**
life	*boat, belt, -guard, -jacket, -saving*
lift	*ed, ing, er, s*
light	*er, est, ly, ness, weight, s*
light	*ed, ing, ish, er, house, ship, s*
lighten	*ed, ing, s*
lightning	*-conductor*
like	*able, d, ∉ing, ness, s*
likel *y*	*ier, iest, ihood*
lilac	*-tree, s*
lil *y*	*ies*
limb	*less, s*
lime	*-juice, light, -tree, s*
limit	*ed, ing, less, s*
limp	*ed, ing, er, est, ly, ness, s*
limpet	*s*
line	*d, ∉ing, sman, smen, s*
linen	*s*
liner	*s*
linger	*ed, ing, er, s*
link	*ed, ing, s*
linoleum or **lino**	*s*
lion	*-tamer, s*
lioness	*es*
lip	*-reading, stick, s*
liquid	*s*
liquorice or **licorice**	
list	*ed, ing, s*
listen	*ed, ing, er, s*
lit or **lighted**	
literature	
litter	*ed, ing, -basket, -bin, -bug, -lout, s*
little	*ness*
live	*d, ∉ing, r, s*
livel *y*	*ier, iest, ily, iness*
liver	*ish, s*
lizard	*s*

load	*ed, ing, er, s*
loaf	**loaves**
loan* (lend)	*ed, ing, s*
loathe	*d, ∉ing, s*
loathsome	*ly, ness*
lob	*bed, bing, ber, s*
lobb *y*	*ies*
lobster	*-pot, s*
local	*ly, s*
localit *y*	*ies*
locate	*d, ∉ing, s*
location	*s*
lock	*ed, ing, er, smith, s*
locket	*s*
locomotive	*s*
locust	*s*
lodge	*d, ∉ing, r, s*
loft	*s*
loft *y*	*ier, iest, ily, iness*
log	*ged, ging, -book, -cabin, s*
loganberr *y*	*ies*
loiter	*ed, ing, er, s*
loll	*ed, ing, er, s*
lollipop	*s*
loll *y*	*ies*
lone* (alone)	*r, some*
lonel *y*	*ier, iest, ily, iness*
long	*ed, ing, ingly, er, est, bow, -stop, s*
longitude	*s*
look	*ed, ing, er, -out, s*
looking-glass	*es*
loom	*ed, ing, s*
loop	*ed, ing, hole, s*
loose	*r, st, ly, ness*
loosen	*ed, ing, s*
loot* (plunder)	*ed, ing, er, s*

∉ Drop **e** before adding *ing*

lu   ly ma

lop	ped, ping, -sided, s
lord	ship, s
lorr y	ies
lose	∉ing, r, s
loss	es
lost	
lotion	s
lotto	
loud	er, est, ish, ly, ness, -speaker
lounge	d, ∉ing, r, s
lout	ish, s
love	d, ∉ing, r, bird, -letter, -song, s
lovel y	ier, iest, ily, iness
low	er, est, ly, ness, s
lower	ed, ing, s
lowland	er, s
loyal	ist, ly, ty
lozenge	s

lu

lubricate	d, ∉ing, s
lubrication	
luck	less
luck y	ier, iest, ily, iness
ludo	
lug	ged, ging, s
luggage	-carrier, -rack, -van
lukewarm	ly, ness
lull	ed, ing, s
lullab y	ies
lumbago	s
lumber	ed, ing, er, jack, -room, s
luminous	ly, ness
lump	ed, ing, s
lump y	ier, iest, ily, iness
lunatic	s

lunch	ed, ing, -box, es
luncheon	s
lung	s
lunge	d, ∉ing, s
lupin	s
lurch	ed, ing, es
lure	d, ∉ing, s
lurk	ed, ing, er, s
luscious	ly, ness
lustr e	ous
lust y	ier, iest, ily, iness
lute* (musical instrument)	s
luxuriant	ly
luxurious	ly, ness
luxur y	ies

ly

lying	
lynch	ed, ing, es
lynx	es or **lynx**
lyre* (musical instrument)	s
lyric	al, s

ma

macaroni	
mace	-bearer, s
machine	d, ∉ing, -gun, s
machinery	
machinist	s
mackerel	s or **mackerel**
mackintosh	es
mad	der, dest, ly, ness, house, man, men
madden	ed, ing, s
madam	s
madame (French)	**mesdames**

∉ Drop **e** before adding *ing*

*	lute	lyre
	loot	liar

made* (make)		**maniac**	s
magazine	s	**manicure**	d, øing, s
maggot	y, s	**manner*** (way; behaviour)	ed, s
magic	al, ally	**manoeuvre**	d, øing, s
magician	s	**manor*** (lord's land)	-house, s
magistrate	s	**mansion**	s
magnet	ic, ically, ism, s	**mantelpiece**	s
magnetize	d, øing, s	**manual**	ly, s
magnificent	ly	**manufacture**	d, øing, r, s
magnify	ing	**manure**	d, øing, s
magnif ied	ies	**manuscript**	s
magpie	s	**many**	
maid* (girl)	en, servant, s	**map** ped, ping, per, -reading, s	
mail* (armour; post)	ed, ing, -bag, s	**marble**	s
maim	ed, ing, s	**March**	es
main* (chief)	ly, land, stay, s	**march**	ed, ing, es
maintain	ed, ing, s	**mare*** (female horse)	s
maison(n)ette	s	**margarine**	s
maize* (corn)		**margin**	s
majest y	ic, ically, ies	**marigold**	s
major	ette, -general, s	**marine**	r, s
majorit y	ies	**marionette**	s
make øing, -believe, shift, -up, r, s		**mark** ed, ing, sman, smen, er, s	
malaria		**market** ed, ing, -day, -place, -stall, s	
male* (man; masculine)	s	**marmalade**	s
mallet	s	**maroon**	ed, ing, s
mammal	s	**marquee**	s
mammoth	s	**marriage**	s
man ned, ning, hole, hood, **men**		**marry**	ing
manl y ier, iest, ily, iness		**marr** ied	ies
manage d, øing, able, ably, ment, s		**marrow**	s
manager	s	**Mars**	
manageress	es	**marsh**	es
mandolin	s	**marsh** y ier, iest, iness	
mane* (hair)	s	**marshal**	led, ling, s
manger	s	**marsh-mallow**	s
mangle	d, øing, s	**martyr** ed, ing, dom, s	

ø Drop **e** before adding *ing*

me

marvel	led, ling, s
marvellous	ly, ness
marzipan	
mascot	s
masculine	s
mash	ed, ing, es
mask	ed, ing, s
mason	ry, s
masquerade	d, ǿing, r, s
mass	ed, ing, es
massacre	d, ǿing, s
massage	d, ǿing, s
masseur	s
masseuse	s
massive	ly, ness
mast	ed, -head, s
master	ed, ing, ly, y, mind, piece, s
mat	ted, ting, s
matador	s
match	ed, ing, sticks, wood, box, es
mate	d, ǿing, s
material	s
mathematic	al, ally, ian, s
matinée	s
matron	s
matter	ed, ing, s
mattress	es
maul	ed, ing, s
mauve	r, st, s
maximum	a
may	be
May	s
maypole	s
mayonnaise	
mayor* (head of town or city)	s
mayoress	es
maze* (puzzle)	s

me

meadow	s
meagre	ly, ness
meal	-time, s
mean	er, est, ly, ness, s
meaning	less, s
meant	
meantime	
meanwhile	
measles	
measure	d, ǿing, ment, s
meat* (flesh)	y, -axe, -ball, -pie, s
mechanic	al, ally, s
mechanism	s
mechanize	d, ǿing, s
medal* (badge—for bravery, etc.)	s
medallion	s
meddle* (interfere)	d, ǿing, some, r, s
medi(a)eval	
medical	ly, s
medicine	s
Mediterranean	
medium	s or **media**
meek	er, est, ly, ness
meet* (come together)	ing, s
megaphone	s
melody	ious, iously, ies
melon	s
melt	ed, ing, s
member	ship, s
memorial	s
memorize	d, ǿing, s
memory	ies
menace	d, ǿing, s
menagerie	s
mend	ed, ing, er, s
mental	ity, ly

ǿ Drop **e** before adding *ing*

*	maze	mayor	meat	medal
	maize	mare	meet	meddle

mi

mention	*ed, ing, s*
menu	*s*
merchant	*s*
merciful	*ly, ness*
merciless	*ly, ness*
merc *y*	*ies*
mercury	
mere	*ly*
meringue	*s*
merit	*ed, ing, s*
mermaid	*s*
merr *y*	*ier, iest, ily, iment*
mesmerize	*d, ¢ing, s*
mess	*ed, ing, es*
mess *y*	*ier, iest, ily, iness*
message	*s*
messenger	*s*
metal	*lic, work, -detector, s*
meteor	*ic, ite, oid, ology, ologist, s*
meter* (measuring box)	*s*
method	*ical, ically, s*
methylated spirit(s)	
metre* (length measure)	*s*
mew	*ed, ing, s*

mi·

miaow	*ed, ing, s*
mice	
microphone	*s*
microscope	*s*
midday	
middle	*-aged, -class*
midge	*s*
midget	*s*
midnight	
midst	
midway	

might	
might *y*	*ier, iest, ily, iness*
migrate	*d, ¢ing, s*
migration	*s*
mild	*er, est, ly, ness*
mildew	*ed, ¢ing, s*
mile	*age, stone, s*
military	
milk	*ed, ing, er, man, men, -shake, s*
milk *y*	*ier, iest, ily, iness*
mill	*ed, ing, er, -pond, stone, s*
millimetre	*s*
million	*th, s*
millionaire	*s*
millionairess	*es*
mime	*d, ¢ing, s*
mimic	*ked, king, s*
mince	*d, ¢ing, r, meat, -pie, s*
mind*	*ed, ing, er, ful, less, -reader, s*
mine *d,* ¢ing, field, sweeper, s*	
miner* (mine worker)	*s*
mineral	*s*
mingle	*d, ¢ing, s*
miniature	*s*
minim *um*	*a*
minister	*s*
minnow	*s*
minor* (young person; lesser)	*s*
minstrel	*s*
mint	*ed, ing, y, -sauce, s*
minus	*es*
minute	*-hand, s*
minute (small)	*ly, ness*
miracle	*s*
miraculous	*ly, ness*
mirage	*s*
mirror	*ed, ing, s*

¢ Drop **e** before adding *ing*

*	meter	mind	miner
	metre	mined	minor

mo

mirth	
misbehave	d, ∉ing, s
misbehaviour	
mischief	-maker
mischievous	ly, ness
miser	ly, s
miserabl e	y
miser y	ies
misfortune	s
mishap	s
mislay	ing, s
mislaid	
misplace	d, ∉ing, s
miss	ed*, ing, es
missile	s
mission	s
missionar y	ies
mist* (haze; fog)	ed, ing, s
mist y	ier, iest, ily, iness
mistake	n, ∉ing, s
mistook	
mistletoe	
mistress	es
mistrust	ed, ing, s
mitten	s
mix	ed, ing, es
mixer	s
mixture	s

mo

moan* (groan)	ed, ing, er, s
moat	ed, s
mob	bed, bing, s
mobile	s
moccasin	s
mock	ed, ing, s

mocker y	ies
model	led, ling, ler, s
moderate	d, ∉ing, ly, ness, s
modern	ity, ly, ness, s
modernize	d, ∉ing, s
modest	ly, y
moist	ure, ly, ness
moisten	ed, ing, s
mole	hill, skin, s
moment	s
monarch	s
monaster y	ies
Monday	s
money	-lender, -order, -spider, s
mongrel	s
monitor	s
monitress	es
monk	s
monkey	-nut, s
monotonous	ly, ness
monster	s
month	s
monthl y	ies
monument	s
mood	s
mood y	ier, iest, ily, iness
moon	beam, less, light, s
moor	hen, land, s
moor	age, ed, ing, s
mop	ped, ping, per, head, s
moral	ly, s
more	over
morning* (a.m.)	s
morsel	s
mortal	ly, s
mortar	-board, s
mosaic	s

∉ Drop **e** before adding *ing*

mu   my

mosquito	es
moss	es
moss y	ier, iest, iness
most	ly
motel	s
moth	-eaten, -proof, ball, s
mother	ed, ing, less, ly, hood, s
motion	ed, ing, less, -picture, s
motor	ed, ing, -bike, -boat, -car, ist, s
motor	-cycle, -cyclist, -scooter, way, s
motto	es
mould	ed, ing, er, s
mould y	ier, iest, iness
moult	ed, ing, s
mound	s
mount	ed, ing, s
mountain	ous, side, -top, s
mountaineer	ing, s
mourn ing* (sorrowing)	ed, ful, fully, er, s
mouse	d, ǿing, ǿy, r, -hole, trap. **mice**
moustache	s
mouth	-organ, ful, s
movable	s
move	d, ǿing, r, ment, s
mow	ed, ing, er, s
mown* (cut grass, etc.)	

mu

much	
mud	-bank, -bath, -flat, guard
mudd y	ier, iest, ily, iness
muddle	d, ǿing, r, s
muffle	d, ǿing, r, s
mulberr y	ies
mule	teer, s
multiplication	

multiply	ing
multipl ied	ier, ies
multitude	s
mumble	d, ǿing, r, s
mumm y	ies
mumps	
munch	ed, ing, es
mural	s
murder	ed, ing, er, s
murderess	es
murmur	ed, ing, er, s
muscle* (of body)	s
museum	s
mushroom	s
music	al, ally, -case, -hall, -stand
musician	s
musket	eer, -shot, s
mussel* (shellfish)	s
must	
mustn't (must not)	
mustard	-pot
must y	ier, iest, ily, iness
mutineer	s
mutiny	ing
mutin ied	ies
mutter	ed, ing, er, s
mutton	-chop, -cutlet
muzzle	d, ǿing, s

my

myrrh	
myself	
myster y	ies
mysterious	ly, ness
mystify	ing
mystif ied	ies

ǿ Drop **e** before adding *ing*

*	mourning	mown		muscle
	morning	moan		mussel

na

nail *ed, ing, -scissors, -file, s*
naked *ly, ness*
name *d, ȩing, ly, less, -plate, sake, s*
nanny *ies*
napkin *-ring, s*
nappy *ies*
narcissus *es* or **narcissi**
narrate *d, ȩing, s*
narrow *ed, ing, er, est, ish, ly, ness, s*
nasturtium *s*
nasty *ier, iest, ily, iness*
nation *al, ally, wide, s*
nationality *ies*
native *s*
nativity *ies*
natural *ly, ness*
naturalist *s*
nature *s*
naughty *ier, iest, ily, iness*
nautical *ly*
naval
nave* (main part of church) *s*
navigate *d, ȩing, s*
navigation
navigator *s*
navy *ies*

ne

near *ed, ing, er, est, ly, ness, s*
neat *er, est, ly, ness*
necessary *ily, ies*
necessity *ies*
neck *lace, let, line, tie, s*
need* (want) *ed, ing, s*
needn't (need not)

needle *work, -case, s*
negative *s*
neglect *ed, ing, s*
neglectful *ly, ness*
Negress *es*
Negro *es*
neigh *ed, ing, s*
neighbour *ing, ly, hood, s*
neither
nephew *s*
nerve *d, ȩing, -racking, s*
nervous *ly, ness*
nest *ed, ing, -egg, ful, s*
nestle *d, ȩing, s*
net *ted, ting, ball, ful, s*
nettle *s*
neutral *s*
never *more, theless*
new* (just made) *er, est, ly, ness*
news *caster, -letter, -reel, -sheet, y*
newsagent *s*
newspaper *man, men, -boy, -girl, s*
newt *s*
next

ni

nibble *d, ȩing, r, s*
nice *r, st, ly, ness*
nick *ed, ing, s*
nickname *d, ȩing, s*
niece *s*
night* *-club, fall, -light, mare, -time, s*
nightingale *s*
nil
nimble *r, st, ness, -footed*
nimbly

ȩ Drop e before adding ing

*	nave	need		new	night
	knave	knead		knew	knight

no   nu ny oa

no

no* (not any; opp. of yes)	*es*
noble	*r, st, man, men, s*
nobody	*ies*
nod	*ded, ding, der, s*
noise	*less, lessly, s*
noisy	*ier, iest, ily, iness*
nomad	*ic, s*
none* (not any)	
nonsense	
noodle	*s*
noon	*day*
noose	*s*
normal	*ly*
Norman	*s*
north	*-east, -west, ern, erly, wards*
nose	*d, ǿing, bag, bleed, dive, gay, s*
nostril	*s*
not* (no)	
notable	*s*
notch	*ed, ing, es*
note	*d, ǿing, book, case, paper, let, s*
nothing	
notice	*d, ǿing, able, ably, -board, s*
notify	*ing*
notified	*ication, ies*
notion	*s*
nougat	
nought	*s*
nourish	*ment, ed, ing, es*
novel	*ist, s*
novelty	*ies*
November	*s*
novice	*s*
now	*adays*
nowhere	
nozzle	*s*

nu

nuclear	
nude	*s*
nudist	*s*
nudge	*d, ǿing, s*
nugget	*s*
nuisance	*s*
numb	*ed, ing, ly, ness, s*
number	*ed, ing, -plate, s*
numeral	*s*
numerical	*ly*
numerous	*ly*
nun* (religious woman)	*s*
nurse	*d, ǿing, maid, s*
nursery	*ies*
nut	*ted, ting, cracker, shell, -tree, s*
nutty	*ier, iest, ily, iness*
nuthatch	*es*
nutmeg	*s*
nutrition	*al, ist*
nutritious	*ly, ness*
nuzzle	*d, ǿing, s*

ny

nylon	*s*
nymph	*s*

oa

oaf* (stupid person)	*ish, s* or **oaves**
oak	*-apple, -tree, s*
oar* (rowing blade)	*sman, smen, s*
oasis	*es*
oast	*-house, s*
oat	*meal, cake, s*
oath* (promise; swear-word)	*s*

ǿ Drop **e** before adding *ing*

*	no	none	not		oaf	oar
	know	nun	knot		oath	ore
						or

ob

obedience	
obedient	*ly*
obey	*ed, ing, s*
object	*ed, ing, or, s*
objection	*able, ably, s*
obligation	*s*
oblige	*d, ǿing, s*
obliterate	*d, ǿing, s*
oblong	*s*
oboe	*ǿist, s*
obscure	*d, ǿing, ly, s*
obscurity	
observant	*ly*
observation	*s*
observatory	*ies*
observe	*d, ǿing, r, s*
obstacle	*-course, -race, s*
obstinate	*ly*
obstruct	*ed, ing, ion, s*
obtain	*able, ed, ing, s*
obvious	*ly, ness*

oc

occasion	*al, ally, s*
occupant	*s*
occupation	*s*
occupy	*ing*
occup*ied*	*ier, ies*
occur	*red, ring, rence, s*
ocean	*s*
o'clock	
octagon	*al, s*
October	*s*
octopus	*es* or **octopodes**
oculist	*s*

od

odd	*er, est, ly, ness, ment, s*
odious	*ly, ness*
odour	*s*

of

of	
off	*ing, hand, chance, -side, spring*
offence	*s*
offend	*ed, ing, er, s*
offensive	*ly, ness*
offer	*ed, ing, s*
offertor*y*	*ies*
office	*-block, -boy, -girl, -worker, s*
officer	*s*
official	*ly, s*
often	*er, est*

og

ogre	*s*
ogress	*es*

oi

oil	*ed, ing, can, -rig, -stove, -well, s*
oil	*-heater, -painting, skin, -tanker, s*
oil*y*	*ier, iest, ily, iness*
ointment	*s*

ol

old	*en, er, est, ish, -time*
old-fashioned	*ness*
olive	*-oil, -grove, -tree, s*
Olympic Games or **Olympics**	

ǿ Drop e before adding ing

om on op   or os ot

om

omelet(te)	s
omen	s
omission	s
omit	ted, ting, s
omnibus	es

on

once	
oncoming	
one*	self, -sided, s
onion	y, -skin, s
onlooker	s
only	
onslaught	s
onto	
onward	s

op

opal	s
opaque	ly, ness
open	ed, ing, ly, ness, er, s
opera	-glasses, -house, -singer, s
operatic	s
operate	d, éing, s
operation	s
operator	s
opinion	s
opponent	s
opportunit y	ies
oppose	d, éing, s
opposite	ly, ness
opposition	
optician	s
optimist	ic, ically, s

or

oral	ly
orange	ade, -blossom, -peel, -tree, s
orang-(o)utan	s
orator	s
orbit	ed, ing, s
orchard	s
orchestra	l, s
orchid	s
ordeal	s
order	ed, ing, s
orderl y	iness, ies
ordinar y	ily, iness
ore* (metal in rock)	s
organ	-grinder, -loft, -pipe, ist, s
organization	s
organize	d, éing, r, s
orient	
oriental	s
origin	s
original	ity, ly
originate	d, éing, s
ornament	ed, ing, al, ation, s
ornithologist	s
ornithology	
orphan	ed, ing, age, s

os

osier	s
ostrich	es

ot

other	s
otherwise	
otter	s

é Drop **e** before adding *ing*

*	one (1)	ore
	won	oar
		or

ou ov   ow ox oy

ou	
ought	
ounce	s
our* (belonging to us)	s
ourselves	
out come, let, look, put, right, standing	
outbreak	s
outburst	s
outcast	s
outer	most
outfit	ted, ting, ter, s
outhouse	s
outing	s
outlaw	ed, ing, s
outline	d, ǿing, s
outnumber	ed, ing, s
out-patient	s
outpost	s
outrage	d, ǿing, s
outrageous	ly, ness
outside	r, s
outskirts	
outward	ly, ness, s
outwit	ted, ting, s

ov	
oval	s
oven	s
over	s
overall	s
overbalance	d, ǿing, s
overboard	
overcame	
overcome	ǿing, s
overcoat	s
overcrowd	ed, ing, s

overdose	d, ǿing, s
overflow	ed, ing, s
overhaul	ed, ing, s
overhead	s
overhear	ing, s
overheard	
overjoyed	
overlap	ped, ping, s
overload	ed, ing, s
overlook	ed, ing, s
overpower	ed, ing, s
overseas	
oversleep	ing, s
overslept	
overtake	n, ǿing, s
overtook	
overthrow	n, ing, s
overthrew	
overtime	
overturn	ed, ing, s
overwhelm	ed, ing, s
overwork	ed, ing, s

ow	
owe	d, ǿing, s
owl	et, s
own	ed, ing, er, s

ox	
ox	en
oxlip	s
oxygen	

oy	
oyster -bed, -catcher, -farm, -shell, s	

ǿ Drop **e** before adding *ing*.

*	our
	hour

pa

pa	
pace	d, ǿing, r, s
Pacific	
pack	ed, ing, er, s
package	d, ǿing, s
packet	ed, ing, s
pad	ded, ding, der, s
paddle	d, ǿing, r, -boat, -steamer, s
padlock	ed, ing, s
page	-boy, s
pageant	s
paid	
pail* (bucket)	ful, s
pain* (suffering)	ed, ing, -killer, s
painful	ly, ness
painless	ly, ness
paint	ed, ing, er, s
pair* (two)	ed, ing, s
palace	s
pale* (faint; whitish)	r, st, ly, ness, s
palette	s
palm	-tree, s
pamper	ed, ing, er, s
pamphlet	s
pan	ned, ning, ful, cake, s
panda	s
pane* (sheet of glass)	s
panel	led, ling, list, s
panic	ked, king, ky, -stricken, -struck, s
panorama	s
pans y	ies
pant	ed, ing, s
panther	s
pantomime	s
pantr y	ies
paper	ed, ing, -boy, -girl, -chain, -clip, s
papier mâché	

parachute	d, ǿing, -troops, s
parade	d, ǿing, -ground, s
paraffin	-heater, -oil
parallel	ed, ing, s
paralyse	d, ǿing, s
paralys is	es
paratroops	
parcel	led, ling, s
parch	ed, ing, es
parchment	s
pardon	able, ed, ing, s
pare* (cut away; peel)	d, ǿing, s
parent	age, al, s
parish	es
park	ed, ing, land, -keeper, s
parliament	s
parrot	s
parsley	-sauce
parsnip	s
parson	age, s
part	ed, ing, ly, s
particle	s
particular	ly, s
partition	ed, ing, s
partner	ed, ing, ship, s
partridge	s
part y	ies
pass	ed*, ing, able, es
passage	way, s
passenger	s
passion	ate, ately, s
passport	s
password	s
past* (time gone by)	
paste	d, ǿing, s
pastel* (crayon)	led, ling, s
pastille* (sweet)	s

ǿ Drop **e** before adding *ing*

*	pail	pain	pair	passed	pastel
	pale	pane	pare	past	pastille
			pear		

pe

pastime	s	**peck**	ed, ing, er, s
pastr y	ies	**peculiar**	ly
pasture	d, ǿing, s	**peculiarit** y	ies
past y	ies	**pedal*** (foot-lever)	led, ling, -cycle, s
pat	ted, ting, s	**peddle*** (to hawk goods)	d, ǿing, s
patch	ed, ing, work, es	**pedestrian**	s
patch y	ier, iest, ily, iness	**pedigree**	s
path	way, s	**pedlar**	s
pathetic	ally	**peel*** (skin of fruit)	ed, ing, er, s
patience		**peep**	ed, ing, er, -hole, -show, s
patient	ly, s	**peer*** (stare)	ed, ing, s
patrol	led, ling, man, men, -leader, s	**peg**	ged, ging, s
patter	· ed, ing, s	**Pekin(g)ese**	**Pekin(g)ese**
pattern	ed, ing, -book, s	**pelican**	s
pause* (hesitate)	d, ǿing, s	**pellet**	s
pave	d, ǿing, ment, s	**pelt**	ed, ing, s
pavilion	s	**pen**	ned, ning, -friend, -nib, s
paw (animal's foot)	s,* ed, ing	**penalt** y	ies
pawn	ed, ing, broker, shop, -ticket, s	**pence**	
pay	able, ing, er, ment, -day, -desk, s	**pencil**	led, ling, -case, -sharpener, s
paid		**pendulum**	s
		penetrate	d, ǿing, s
## pe		**penguin**	s
		peninsula	s
pea	nut, -pod, -soup, -shooter, s	**pen** knife	knives
peace* (quiet)	able, -offering, -time	**pennant**	s
peaceful	ly, ness	**penn** y	ies or **pence**
peach	es	**penniless**	ly, ness
peacock	s	**pension**	ed, ing, able, er, -book, s
peahen	s	**people**	s
peak	ed, ing, s	**pepper**	ed, ing, y, -pot, mint, s
peal* (sound of bells)	ed, ing, s	**perambulator**	s
pear* (fruit)	-drop, -tree, s	**perch**	ed, ing, es
pearl	-diver, -fisher, s	**percussion**	-band, s
peasant	ry, s	**perfect**	ly, ed, ing, ion, s
peat	-bog, -moor, y	**perform**	ed, ing, ance, er, s
pebble	-stone, s	**perfume**	d, ǿing, s
pebbl y	ier, iest, iness		

ǿ Drop **e** before adding *ing*

*	pause	peace	pear	peal	pedal	peer
	paws	piece	pair	peel	peddle	pier
			pare			

ph

pi

perhaps	
peril	*ous, ously, s*
period	*ic, ical, ically, s*
periscope	*s*
perish	*ed, ing, es*
permanent	*ly*
permission	
permit	*ted, ting, s*
perplex	*ed, ing, es*
persevere	*d, ẹing, ẹance, s*
persist	*ed, ing, ence, ent, s*
person	*al, ally, s*
perspiration	
perspire	*d, ẹing, s*
persuade	*d, ẹing, s*
persuasion	
persuasive	*ly, ness*
pessimist	*ic, ically, s*
pester	*ed, ing, s*
pet	*ted, ting, -shop, s*
petal	*s*
petrol	*eum, -pump, -station, s*
petticoat	*s*
pew	*s*
pewter	

ph

phantom	*s*
pheasant	*s*
philatelist	*s*
phone	*d, ẹing. -booth, s*
photo	*-fit, -frame, s*
photograph	*ed, ing, y, er, s*
physical	*ly*
physician	*s*
physics	

pi

pi* ($\pi = 3.14159$)	
pianist	*s*
piano	*-accordion, -stool, s*
piccolo	*-player, s*
pick	*ed, ing, er, axe, pocket, s*
pickle	*d, ẹing, r, s*
picnic	*ked, king, ker, -basket, s*
picture	*d, ẹing, -book, -frame, s*
picturesque	*ly, ness*
pie*	*crust, -shop, s*
piece* (a part)	*d, ẹing, s*
pier* (jetty)	*s*
pierce	*d, ẹing, s*
pierrot	*s*
pig	*let, skin, s*
pigst *y*	*ies*
pigeon	*-hole, -house, -loft, s*
pigm *y* or **pygm** *y*	*ies*
pigtail	*s*
pike	*man, men, staff, s*
pilchard	*s*
pile	*d, ẹing, s*
pilgrim	*age, s*
pillar	*s*
pillar-box	*es*
pillion	*-rider, -seat, s*
pillow	*case, slip, -fight, s*
pilot	*ed, ing, s*
pimple	*d, ẹing, s*
pimpl *y*	*ier, iest, iness*
pin	*ned, ning, cushion, s*
pincers	**pincers**
pinch	*ed, ing, es*
pine	*d, ẹing, apple, -cone, -needle, -tree, s*
pink	*er, est, ish, y, ness, s*
pint	*s*

ẹ Drop **e** before adding *ing*

*	pi	piece	pier
	pie	peace	peer

pl

pioneer	ed, ing, s
pipe	d, ǿing, r, -cleaner, ful, s
piranha	s
pirate	s
pistil* (part of flower)	s
pistol* (small gun)	-shot, s
pit	ted, ting, fall, -head, -prop, s
pitch	ed, ing, -black, -dark, es
pitchfork	ed, ing, s
piteous	ly
pity	ing
pitied	iful, iless, ies
pixie	s or **pix**y, ies
pizza	s

pl

placard	s
place* (position)	d, ing, s
plague	d, ǿing, s
plaice* (fish)	**plaice**
plain*	er, est, ly, ness, s
plait	ed, ing, s
plan	ned, ning, ner, s
plane* (tool; to smooth)	d, ǿing, s
plane* (aeroplane; tree)	s
planet	s
plank	ed, ing, s
plant	ed, ing, ation, er, s
plaster	ed, ing, er, s
plastic	s
plasticine	
plate	d, ǿing, ful, -glass, -rack, s
platform	s
platinum	
play	ed, ing, ground, mate, time, er, s
play	-group, -pen, thing, wright, s
playful	ly, ness

po

plead	ed, ing, s
pleasant	ly, ness
please	d, ǿing, s
pleasure	s
pleat	ed, ing, s
plentiful	ly, ness
plenty	
pliers	**pliers**
plimsoll	s
plod	ded, ding, der, s
plot	ted, ting, ter, s
plough	ed, ing, man, men, boy, s
pluck	ed, ing, er, s
plucky	ier, iest, ily, iness
plug	ged, ging, ger, s
plum*	-pudding, -stone, -tree, s
plumage	
plumb*	ed, ing, -line, s
plumber	s
plump	er, est, ly, ness
plunder	ed, ing, er, s
plunge	d, ǿing, r, s
plural	s
plus	es

po

poach	ed, ing, es
poacher	s
pocket	ed, ing, -book, -money, ful, s
pocket-knife	-knives
podgy	ier, iest, ily, iness
poem	s
poet	ic, ical, ically, s
poetry	
point	ed, ing, -blank, -duty, less, er,'s
poise	d, ǿing, s
poison	ed, ing, ous, ously, er, s

ǿ Drop **e** before adding *ing*

*	pistil	place	plain	plum
	pistol	plaice	plane	plumb

poke	*d, ∅ing, r, s*	**portable**	*s*
polar bear	*s*	**porter**	*s*
pole* (long rod)	*-jump, -vault, s*	**porthole**	*s*
police	*d, ∅ing, -officer, man, woman*	**portion**	*ed, ing, s*
police force	*s*	**portrait**	*s*
police station	*s*	**pose**	*d, ∅ing, s*
polish	*ed, ing, es*	**position**	*ed, ing, s*
polite	*r, st, ly, ness*	**positive**	*ly, ness*
political	*ly*	**possess**	*ed, ing, ive, es*
politician	*s*	**possession**	*s*
poll* (vote)	*ed, ing, s*	**possibilit**y	*ies*
pollen		**possible**	*s*
polo	*-stick*	**possibly**	
polytechnic	*s*	**post**	*ed, ing, man, men, card, mark, s*
polythene		**postage**	*-stamp*
pomp	*ous, ously, osity*	**postal order**	*s*
pond	*-life, -snail, weed, s*	**poster**	*s*
ponder	*ed, ing, s*	**post office**	*s*
pontoon	*-bridge, s*	**postpone**	*d, ∅ing, ment, s*
pony	*ies*	**pos**y	*ies*
poodle	*s*	**pot**	*ted, ting, ful, -luck, -hole, -shot, s*
pool	*ed, ing, s*	**potato**	*es*
poor* (not rich)	*er, est, ly, ness*	**potion**	*s*
pop	*ped, ping, per, corn, gun, s*	**potter**	*ed, ing, s*
pop	*-group, -music, -singer, -song, s*	**potter**y.	*ies*
poplar	*-tree, s*	**pouch**	*es*
poppy	*ies*	**poultice**	*d, ∅ing, s*
popular	*ity, ly*	**poultry**	*-farm*
population		**pounce**	*d, ∅ing, s*
porcelain		**pound**	*ed, ing, s*
porch	*es*	**pour*** (flow out)	*ed, ing, er, s*
porcupine	*s*	**pout**	*ed, ing, er, s*
pore* (study; tiny hole)	*d, ∅ing, s*	**poverty**	*-stricken*
pork	*-butcher, -chop, -pie, er, y*	**powder**	*ed, ing, y, -puff, -room, s*
porpoise	*s*	**power**	*ed, -house, -plant, -station, s*
porridge		**powerful**	*ly, ness*
port	*s*	**powerless**	*ly, ness*

∅ Drop **e** before adding *ing*

*	pole	poor
	poll	pore
		pour

pra pre   pri   pro

pr	
practical	ly, ity, ness
practice* (noun)	s
practise* (verb)	d, ǿing, s
prairie	s
praise	d, ǿing, s
prance	d, ǿing, s
prank	ster, s
prawn	ed, ing, er, s
pray* (ask God)	ed, ing, s
prayer	-book, -meeting, s
preach	ed, ing, es
preacher	s
precaution	ary, s
precious	ly, ness
precipice	s
prefect	s
prefer	red, ring, able, ably, ence, s
prehistoric	al, ally
preliminary	ies
premises	
preparation	s
prepare	d, ǿing, s
prescribe	d, ǿing, s
prescription	s
presence	
present	ed, ing, ation, s
presently	
preserve	d, ǿing, s
president	s
press	ed, ing, es
pressure	-cooker, -gauge, s
pretend	ed, ing, er, s
pretty	ier, iest, ily, iness
prevent	ed, ing, ion, s
previous	ly, ness
prey* (victim; thing hunted)	ed, ing, s

price	d, ǿing, less, -list, -tag, s
prick	ed, ing, er, s
prickle	d, ǿing, s
prickly	ier, iest, iness
pride* (proudness)	d, ǿing, s
pried* (looked into)	
priest	ly, hood, s
priestess	es
primary school	s
primitive	ly, ness
primrose	s
prince	ly, s
princess	es
principal* (head; chief)	ly, s
principle* (rule; truth)	s
print	ed, ing, er, s
prison	er, s
private	ly, s
privilege	d, ǿing, s
prize	d, ǿing, -winner, s
probability	ies
probable	s
probably	
problem	s
procedure	s
proceed	ed, ing, s
process	ed, ing, es
procession	s
proclaim	ed, ing, s
procure	d, ǿing, s
prod	ded, ding, s
produce	d, ǿing, r, s
product	ive, ion, s
profession	al, ally, s
professor	s
profit* (gain)	able, ed, ing, eer, s
programme	d, ǿing, r, s

*ǿ Drop **e** before adding ing*

*	practice	pray	pride	principal	profit
	practise	prey	pried	principle	prophet

pru pry   pu

progress	*ed, ing, es*	**pu**	
prohibit	*ed, ing, s*	**public**	*ly, -house*
project	*ed, ing, ile, ion, or, s*	**publication**	*s*
promenade	*d, ø̸ing, r, s*	**publicity**	
prominent	*ly*	**publish**	*ed, ing, es*
promise	*d, ø̸ing, s*	**publisher**	*s*
promote	*d, ø̸ing, r, s*	**pudding**	*s*
promotion	*s*	**puddle**	*s*
prompt	*ed, ing, er, est, ly, ness, s*	**puff**	*ed, ing, er, s*
pronounce	*d, ø̸ing, ment, s*	**puff** *y*	*ier, iest, ily, iness*
proof	*s*	**pull**	*ed, ing, er, s*
prop	*ped, ping, s*	**pullover**	*s*
propel	*led, ling, ler, s*	**pulley**	*-block, s*
proper	*ly*	**pulp**	*ed, ing, er, s*
propert *y*	*ies*	**pulpit**	*s*
prophec *y* (noun)	*ies*	**pulse**	*d, ø̸ing, s*
prophes *y* (verb)	*ied, ies*	**pump**	*ed, ing, s*
prophesying		**pumpkin**	*s*
prophet* (foreteller of future) *s*		**punch**	*ed, ing, es*
proposal	*s*	**punctual**	*ity, ly*
propose	*d, ø̸ing, r, s*	**puncture**	*d, ø̸ing, s*
proprietor	*s*	**punish**	*able, ed, ing, es*
prosecute	*d, ø̸ing, s*	**punishment**	*s*
prosper	*ed, ing, ous, ously, ity, s*	**punt**	*ed, ing, er, s*
protect	*ed, ing, ion, ive, or, s*	**pupa**	*e*
protest	*ed, ing, s*	**pupil**	*s*
Protestant	*s*	**puppet**	*ry, -play, -show, s*
protrude	*d, ø̸ing, s*	**pupp** *y*	*ies*
proud	*er, est, ly*	**purchase**	*d, ø̸ing, r, s*
prove	*d, ø̸ing, s*	**pure**	*r, st, ly, ness*
proverb	*s*	**purity**	
provide	*d, ø̸ing, r, s*	**purple**	*r, st, ness, s*
provision	*ed, ing, s*	**purpose**	*ly, s*
prowl	*ed, ing, er, s*	**purr**	*ed, ing, s*
prune	*d, ø̸ing, s*	**purse**	*r, -snatcher, s*
pry	*ing*	**pursue**	*d, ø̸ing, r, s*
pr *ied**	*ies*	**pursuit**	*s*

*ø̸ Drop **e** before adding ing*

*	prophet	pried
	profit	pride

push	ed, ing, es
puss y	ies
put	ting, s
putt (golf)	ed, ing, er, s
putting-green	s
putty	
puzzle	d, ǿing, r, ment, s

py

pygm y or **pigm** y	ies
pyjamas	
pylon	s
pyramid	s
python	s

qua

quack	ed, ing, s
quadrangle	s
quadruplet	s
quaint	er, est, ly, ness
quake	d, ǿing, s
qualification	s
qualify	ing
qualif ied	ies
qualit y	ies
quantit y	ies
quarantine	d, ǿing, s
quarrel	led, ling, ler, some, s
quarry	ing
quarr ied	ies
quart (two pints)	s*
quarter	ed, ing, s
quartet(te)	s
quartz* (rock-crystal)	
quay* (wharf)	side, s

que

queen	s
queer	er, est, ly, ness
quell	ed, ing, s
quench	ed, ing, es
query	ing
quer ied	ies
quest	ed, ing, s
question	ed, ing, er, -master, s
queue* (line of persons, etc.)	d, r, s
queueing or **quiuing**	

qui

quibble	d, ǿing, r, s
quick	er, est, ly, ness
quicken	ed, ing, s
quiet	ed, ing, er, est, ly, ness, s
quieten	ed, ing, s
quill	s
quilt	ed, ing, s
quince	s
quinine	
quintet(te)	s
quintuplet	s
quire* (measure of paper)	s
quit	ted, ting, ter, s
quite	
quiver	ed, ing, s
quiz	zed, zing, zes

quo

quoit	s
quota	s
quotation	-mark, s
quote	d, ǿing, s

ǿ Drop **e** before adding *ing*

ra

re_a

ra	
rabbit	ed, ing, er, -hole, -warren, s
race	d, ǿing, r, course, horse, track, s
rack	ed, ing, s
racket* (noise)	ed, ing, eer, s
racket* or **racquet*** (bat)	s
radar	
radiate	d, ǿing, s
radiator	s
radio	ed, ing, s
radish	es
radius	i
raffle	d, ǿing, r, -ticket, s
raft	s
rafter	s
rag	ged, ging, s
ragged	ly, ness
rage	d, ǿing, s
raid	ed, ing, er, s
rail	ing, s
railway	-carriage, -crossing, -line, s
rain*	ed, ing, -water, bow, coat, drop, s
rainy	ier, iest, ily, iness
raise* (lift up)	d, ǿing, s
raisin	s
rake	d, ǿing, r, s
rally	ing
rallied	ies
ram	med, ming, rod, s
ramble	d, ǿing, r, s
ramshackle	
ranch	es
rancher	s
random	ly
rang	
range	d, ǿing, r, s
rank	ed, ing, s

ransack	ed, ing, er, s
ransom	ed, ing, s
rap* (knock)	ped, ping, s
rapid	ity, ly, s
rare	r, st, ly, ness
rascal	ly, s
rash	er, est, ly, ness
rasher	s
raspberry	ies
rat	ted, ting, -hole, -poison, -trap, s
rate	d, ǿing, payer, s
rather	
ration	ed, ing, s
rattle	d, ǿing, r, snake, s
rave	d, ǿing, s
raven	s
ravenous	ly, ness
ravine	s
raw	er, est, ly, ness
ray (beam of light)	s*
razor	-blade, -edge, -shell, s
re	
reach	ed, ing, es
react	ed, ing, ion, or, s
read*	ing, er, s
ready	ier, iest, ily, iness
real* (true)	ly, ist, istic, ism
reality	ies
realize	d, ǿing, s
really	
reap	ed, ing, er, s
reappear	ed, ing, ance, s
rear	ed, ing, guard, -lamp, -light, ward, s
rearrange	d, ǿing, ment, s
reason	ed, ing, able, ably, s

ǿ Drop **e** before adding *ing*

*****	racket	rain	raise	rap	read	read	real
	racquet	reign	rays	wrap	reed	red	reel
		rein					

reb   rec   red   ree   ref   reg   reh   rei   rej   rel

rebel	led, ling, s	**refer**	red, ring, s
rebellion	s	**referee**	d, ing, s
rebellious	ly, ness	**reference**	-book, s
rebound	ed, ing, s	**reflect**	ed, ing, ion, or, s
recall	ed, ing, s	**refrain**	ed, ing, s
recapture	d, øing, s	**refresh**	ed, ing, es
receipt	ed, ing, -book, s	**refreshment**	s
receive	d, øing, r, s	**refrigerator**	s
recent	ly, ness	**refuge**	s
receptacle	s	**refugee**	s
reception	ist, s	**refund**	ed, ing, s
recess	ed, ing, es	**refusal**	s
recipe	s	**refuse**	d, øing, s
recital	s	**regain**	ed, ing, s
recitation	s	**regard**	ed, ing, less, lessly, s
recite	d, øing, s	**regatta**	s
reckless	ly, ness	**regiment**	ed, ing, al, s
reckon	ed, ing, er, s	**region**	al, s
recognize	d, øing, s	**register**	ed, ing, s
recollect	ed, ing, ion, s	**regret**	ted, ting, table, tably, s
recommend	ed, ing, ation, s	**regretful**	ly
record	ed, ing, -player, s	**regular**	ity, ly
recorder	s	**regulate**	d, øing, s
recover	ed, ing, s	**regulation**	s
recover y	ies	**rehearsal**	s
recreation	-ground, s	**rehearse**	d, øing, s
recruit	ed, ing, ment, s	**reign*** (rule)	ed, ing, s
rectangle	s	**rein*** (strap)	ed, ing, s
red* (colour)	der, dest, dish, dy, ness, s	**reindeer**	**reindeer**
redden	ed, ing, s	**reinforce**	d, øing, ment, s
redskin	s	**reject**	ed, ing, ion, s
redecorate	d, øing, s	**rejoice**	d, øing, s
reduce	d, øing, s	**rejoin**	ed, ing, s
reduction	s	**relate**	d, øing, s
reed* (tall grass)	s	**relation**	s
reef	-knot, s	**relative**	s
reel* (spool; dance; stagger)	ed, ing, s	**relax**	ed, ing, es

*ø Drop **e** before adding *ing**

*	red	reed	reel	reign
	read	read	real	rein
				rain

relay	*ed, ing, -race, s*	**request**	*ed, ing, s*
release	*d, ǿing, s*	**require**	*d, ǿing, ment, s*
reliable	*ness*	**rescue**	*d, ǿing, r, s*
relic	*s*	**resemblance**	*s*
relief		**resemble**	*d, ǿing, s*
relieve	*d, ǿing, s*	**reservation**	*s*
religion	*s*	**reserve**	*d, ǿing, s*
religious	*ly, ness*	**reservoir**	*s*
rely	*ing*	**reside**	*d, ǿing, nce, nt, s*
rel*ied*	*iable, ies*	**resign**	*ed, ing, ation, s*
remain	*ed, ing, der, s*	**resist**	*ed, ing, ance, s*
remark	*ed, ing, able, ably, s*	**resolution**	*s*
remed*y*	*ies*	**resort**	*ed, ing, s*
remember	*ed, ing, s*	**respect**	*ed, ing, able, ably, ful, fully, s*
remembrance	*s*	**responsibilit***y*	*ies*
remind	*ed, ing, er, s*	**responsible**	
remnant	*s*	**rest**	*ed, ing, -cure, -home, -room, s*
remote	*ly, ness*	**restful**	*ly, ness*
removal	*s*	**restless**	*ly, ness*
remove	*d, ǿing, r, s*	**restaurant**	*s*
renew	*ed, ing, able, al, s*	**result**	*ed, ing, s*
rent	*ed, ing, able, al, s*	**resume**	*d, ǿing, s*
repair	*ed, ing, able, er, s*	**retire**	*d, ǿing, ment, s*
repay	*ing, able, ment, s*	**retrace**	*d, ǿing, s*
repaid		**retreat**	*ed, ing, s*
repeat	*ed, edly, ing, er, s*	**retrieve**	*d, ǿing, r, s*
repetition	*s*	**return**	*ed, ing, able, -ticket, s*
replace	*d, ǿing, able, ment, s*	**reveal**	*ed, ing, s*
replay	*ed, ing, s*	**revenge**	*d, ǿing, s*
reply	*ing*	**reverse**	*d, ǿing, s*
repl*ied*	*ies*	**review**	*ed, ing, s*
report	*ed, ing, er, s*	**revive**	*d, ǿing, s*
represent	*ed, ing, ative, s*	**revolt**	*ed, ing, s*
reproduce	*d, ǿing, s*	**revolution**	*s*
reptile	*s*	**revolve**	*d, ǿing, s*
republic	*an, s*	**revolver**	*s*
reputation	*s*	**reward**	*ed, ing, s*

*ǿ Drop **e** before adding ing*

rh

rheumatism	
rhinoceros	es
rhododendron	s
rhubarb	
rhyme	d, ǿing, s
rhythm	ic, ical, ically, s

ri

rib	bed, bing, s
ribbon	s
rice	-pudding, -field, s
rich	er, est, ly, ness, es
rick	ed, ing, s
ricket y	iness
ridden	
riddle	d, ǿing, r, s
ride	ǿing, r, s
riding	-crop, -school, -stable, -whip, s
ridge	s
ridicule	d, ǿing, s
ridiculous	ly, ness
rifle	d, ǿing, man, men, -range, -shot, s
rig	ged, ging, ger, s
right* (true; opp. left)	ful, ly, -handed, s
rigid	ity, ly, ness
rim	med, ming, less, s
rind	s
ring* (circle)	ed, ing, leader, -master, s
ring* (bell sound)	ing, er, s
rink	s
rinse	d, ǿing, r, s
riot	ed, ing, er, s
rip	ped, ping, per, -cord, s
ripe	r, st, ly, ness
ripen	ed, ing, s

ripple	d, ǿing, s
rise	ǿing, r, s
risen	
risk	ed, ing, s
risk y	ier, iest, ily, iness
rissole	s
rival	led, ling, s
rivalr y	ies
river	-bank, -bed, -boat, side, s
rivet	ed, ing, er, s

ro

road* (highway)	side, way, -sweeper, s
roam	ed, ing, er, s
roar	ed, ing, er, s
roast	ed, ing, er, s
rob	bed, bing, ber, s
robber y	ies
robe	d, ǿing, s
robin	-redbreast, s
robot	s
rock	ed, ing, -cake, -garden, s
rock y	ier, iest, ily, iness
rocker y	ies
rocket	ed, ing, s
rode* (ride)	
rodeo	s
roe* (deer; fish eggs)	s
rogue	s
rôle* (actor's part)	s
roll* (turn over)	ed, ing, -call, mop, er, s
roller-skate	d, ǿing, r, s
Roman	s
romance	d, ǿing, s
romantic	ally, s
romp	ed, ing, er, s

ǿ Drop **e** before adding *ing*

*				
right	ring	road	roe	rôle
write	wring	rode	row	roll
		rowed		

ru sa

roof	-garden, -rack, -top, s
rook	s
rooker y	ies
room	ful, s
room y	ier, iest, ily, iness
root* (part of a plant)	ed, ing, s
rope	d, ∉ing, -ladder, s
rose	-bud, -garden, -hip, -tree, wood, s
rosette	s
ros y	ier, iest, ily, iness
rot	ted, ting, s
rotate	d, ∉ing, s
rotten	ly, ness
rough	ed, ing, er, est, ly, ness, s
roughen	ed, ing, s
round	ed, ing, ish, ness, sman, smen, s
roundabout	s
rounders	
rouse	d, ∉ing, s
route* (a way)	d, ∉ing, s
routine	s
rove	d, ∉ing, r, s
row (quarrel)	ed, ing, s
row* (line; use oars)	ed,* ing, er, -boat, s
rowing-boat	s
rowd y	ier, iest, ily, iness, ies
royal	ist, ly, ty

ru

rub	bed, bing, s
rubber	-stamp, -tree, s
rubbish	-tip, -heap, y
rubble	
rub y	ies
rucksack	s
rudder	s

rude	r, st, ly, ness
ruffian	s
ruffle	d, ∉ing, s
Rugby	-ball
rugged	ly, ness
ruin	ed, ing, ous, s
rule	d, ∉ing, r, s
rumble	d, ∉ing, s
rummage	d, ∉ing, -sale, s
rumour	ed, ing, s
run	ning, ner, way, s
rung* (ring; ladder step)	s
rural	ly, ness
rush	ed, ing, es
rust	ed, ing, less, -proof, s
rust y	ier, iest, ily, iness
rustle	d, ∉ing, r, s
rut	ted, ting, s
rutt y	ier, iest, iness

sa

sabbath	s
sack	ed, ing, ful, -race, s
sacred	ly, ness
sacrifice	d, ∉ing, s.
sad	der, dest, ly, ness
sadden	ed, ing, s
saddle	d, ∉ing, r, -bag, s
safari	s
safe	r, st, ly, ness, s
safety	-catch, -lamp, -net, -pin, -valve
sag	ged, ging, s
sago	s
said	
sail* (travel by ship)	ed, ing, s
sailor	s

∉ Drop **e** before adding *ing*

*	root	row	rowed	rung	sail
	route	roe	road	wrung	sale
			rode		

SC

saint	s
saintly	ier, iest, ily, iness
sake	s
salad	-dressing, -oil, s
salary	ies
sale* (selling)	sman, smen, -room, s
salmon	**salmon**
saloon	s
salt	ed, ing, -water, -cellar, -spoon, s
salty	ier, iest, iness
salute	d, ɇing, s
salvage	d, ɇing, s
same	ness
sample	d, ɇing, r, s
sanatorium	s or **sanatoria**
sanctuary	ies
sand	-castle, -dune, paper, -storm, s
sandy	ier, iest, iness
sandal	s
sandwich	ed, ing, es
sang	
sank	
Santa Claus	
sap	ped, ping, ling, s
sapphire	s
sarcastic	ally
sardine	s
sash	es
satchel	s
satellite	s
satin	s
satisfaction	
satisfactory	ily, iness
satisfy	ing
satisfied	ies
saturate	d, ɇing, s
Saturday	s

sauce	pan, s
saucer	ful, s
saucy	ier, iest, ily, iness
saunter	ed, ing, s
sausage	-meat, -roll, s
savage	d, ɇing, ly, ry, ness, s
save	d, ɇing, s
saviour	s
saw	ed, ing, dust, mill, s
sawn or **sawed**	
Saxon	s
saxophone	s
say	ing, s
said	

SC

scabbard	s
scaffold	ing, s
scald	ed, ing, s
scale	d, ɇing, s
scalp	ed, ing, s
scamp	ed, ing, s
scamper	ed, ing, s
scan	ned, ning, ner, s
scar	red, ring, s
scarce	r, st, ly, ness
scarcity	ies
scare	d, ɇing, r, crow, s
scarf	-ring, s or **scarves**
scarlet	s
scatter	ed, ing, -brain, s
scavenge	d, ɇing, r, s
scene* (view; place)	-shifter, s
scenery	
scent* (smell; perfume)	ed, ing, s
scheme	d, ɇing, r, s

ɇ Drop **e** before adding *ing*

*
sale
sail

scene
seen

scent
sent

se

scholar	ship, s
scholastic	ally
school	ed, ing, boy, girl, -teacher, s
schoolmaster	s
schoolmistress	es
schooner	s
science	-fiction, s
scientific	ally
scientist	s
scissors	scissors
scold	ed, ing, er, s
scone	s
scoop	ed, ing, er, s
scooter	s
scorch	ed, ing, es
score	d, e̸ing, r, -board, -card, s
scorn	ed, ing, er, s
scornful	ly, ness
scorpion	s
scoundrel	s
scour	ed, ing, er, s
scout	ed, ing, er, master, s
scowl	ed, ing, er, s
scragg y	ier, iest, ily, iness
scramble	d, e̸ing, r, s
scrap	ped, ping, py, -book, -heap, s
scrape	d, e̸ing, r, s
scratch	ed, ing, es
scratch y	ier, iest, ily, iness
scrawl	ed, ing, er, s
scrawl y	ier, iest, iness
scream	ed, ing, er, s
screech	ed, ing, es
screech y	ier, iest, ily, iness
screen	ed, ing, s
screw	ed, ing, driver, s
scribble	d, e̸ing, r, s

scripture	s
scroll	s
scrub	bed, bing, ber, s
scrum	med, ming, mage, s
scuffle	d, e̸ing, r, s
scull* (oar; to row)	ed, ing, er, s
sculler y	ies
sculptor	s
sculptress	es
sculpture	d, e̸ing, s
scuttle	d, e̸ing, s
scythe	d, e̸ing, s

se

sea*	side, sick, shore, front, port, s
sea*	-gull, -horse, -lion, -serpent, s
sea*	man, men, -shell, -water, weed, s
Sea Scout	s
seal	ed, ing, er, skin, s
sealing* (fastening)	-wax
seam* (join; rock vein)	less, s
search	ed, ing, es
searchlight	s
season	-ticket, s
seat	ed, ing, er, -belt, s
seclude	d, e̸ing, s
second	ly, -class, -hand, -rate, s
secondary	
secrecy	
secret	ive, ly, s
secretar y	ies
section	s
secure	d, e̸ing, ly, ness, s
securit y	ies
see* (notice)	ing, s
seed	ed, ing, y, ling, -bed, -cake, s

e̸ Drop **e** before adding *ing*

*	scull	sea	sealing	seam
	skull	see	ceiling	seem

seek	*ing, er, s*	**serpent**	*s*
seem* (appear)	*ed, ing, s*	**servant**	*-girl, s*
seen* (noticed)		**serve**	*d, e̸ing, r, s*
see-saw	*ed, ing, s*	**service**	*d, e̸ing, s*
seize	*d, e̸ing, s*	**serviette**	*s*
seldom		**session**	*s*
select	*ed, ing, ion, s*	**set**	*ting, ter, -square, s*
self	*-conscious, -service,* **selves**	**settee**	*s*
selfish	*ly, ness*	**settle**	*d, e̸ing, r, ment, s*
sell* (exchange for money)	*ing, er,* * *s*	**several**	
sellotape	*d, e̸ing, s*	**severe**	*r, st, ly*
semicircle	*s*	**severity**	
semicircular	*ly*	**sew*** (stitch)	*ed, ing, er, s*
semi-detached		**sewing-machine**	*s*
semolina		**sewn*** (fastened with stitches)	
send	*ing, er, s*	**sextet(te)**	*s*
senior	*s*		
sensation	*al, ally, s*		
sense	*d, e̸ing, s*	**sh**	
senseless	*ly, ness*	**shabb***y*	*ier, iest, ily, iness*
sensible	*ness*	**shack**	*s*
sensibly		**shade**	*d, e̸ing, s*
sent* (send)		**shad***y*	*ier, iest, ily, iness*
sentence	*d, e̸ing, s*	**shadow**	*ed, ing, s*
sentinel	*s*	**shadow***y*	*ily, iness*
sentr*y*	*ies*	**shaft**	*s*
separate	*d, e̸ing, ly, ness, s*	**shagg***y*	*ier, iest, ily, iness*
separation	*s*	**shake**	*n, e̸ing, r, s*
September	*s*	**shak***y*	*ier, iest, ily, iness*
sequin	*s*	**shall**	
serenade	*d, e̸ing, r, s*	**shallow**	*er, est, ly, ness, s*
serf* (villein; slave)	*dom, s*	**shamble**	*d, e̸ing, s*
sergeant	*-major, s*	**shame**	*d, e̸ing, s*
serial* (in parts—as story or film)	*s*	**shameful**	*ly, ness*
series		**shameless**	*ly, ness*
serious	*ly, ness*	**shampoo**	*ed, ing, s*
sermon	*s*	**shamrock**	*s*

e̸ Drop **e** *before adding* ing

*	seem	seen	sell	seller	sent	serf	serial	sew	sewn
	seam	scene	cell	cellar	scent	surf	cereal	sow, so	sown

shandy *ies*	**shingle** *s*
shan't (shall not)	**ship** *ped, ping, load, mate, yard, s*
shanty *ies*	**shipwreck** *ed, ing, s*
shape *d, ∅ing, ly, s*	**shirk** *ed, ing, er, s*
shapeless *ly, ness*	**shirt** *-button, -sleeve, -tail, s*
share *d, ∅ing, s*	**shiver** *ed, ing, y, s*
shark *skin, s*	**shoal** *ed, ing, s*
sharp *er, est, ly, ness, -shooter, s*	**shock** *ed, ing, s*
sharpen *ed, ing, er, s*	**shodd**y *ier, iest, ily, iness*
shatter *ed, ing, s*	**shoe*** *ing, -bag, horn, -lace, maker, s*
shave *n, d, ∅ing, r, s*	**shod**
shawl *s*	**shone**
sheaf **sheaves**	**shoo*** (frighten away) *ed, ing, s*
shear* (cut; clip) *ed, ing, er, s*	**shook**
sheath *s*	**shoot*** (fire) *ing, er, s*
sheath-*knife* *-knives*	**shop** *ped, ping, per, keeper, lifter, s*
shed *ding, der, s*	**shore*** (sea shore) *s*
sheep *-dog, -farmer, -pen, skin,* **sheep**	**shorn**
sheer* (steep)	**short** *age, er, est, ly, ness, bread, s*
sheet *s*	**shorten** *ed, ing, s*
sheik(h) *s*	**shorthand**
shelf **shelves**	**shot** *-gun, s*
shell *ed, ing, er, s*	**should**
shellfish *es or* **shellfish**	**shouldn't** (should not)
she'll (she will; she shall)	**shoulder** *ed, ing, -bag, -blade, -strap, s*
shelter *ed, ing, s*	**shout** *ed, ing, er, s*
shepherd *s*	**shovel** *led, ling, ler, ful, s*
shepherdess *es*	**show** *n, ed, ing, -case, room, s*
sherbet *s*	**show** *-jumping, -ground, s*
sheriff *s*	**shower** *ed, ing, -bath, s*
sherry *ies*	**shower**y *ier, iest, iness*
she's (she is; she has)	**shrank**
shield *ed, ing, s*	**shred** *ded, ding, der, s*
shift *ed, ing, y, er, s*	**shrewd** *er, est, ly, ness*
shin *ned, ning, -guard, -pad, s*	**shriek** *ed, ing, er, s*
shine *∅ing, s*	**shrill** *ed, ing, er, est, y, ness, s*
shiny *ier, iest, ily, iness*	**shrimp** *ed, ing, er, s or* **shrimp**

∅ Drop **e** before adding *ing*

*	shear		shoe	shoot	shore
	sheer		shoo	chute	sure

shrine	s
shrink	ing, able, age, s
shrivel	led, ling, s
shrub	s
shrubber y	ies
shrug	ged, ging, s
shrunk	en
shudder	ed, ing, s
shuffle	d, ⌀ing, r, s
shun	ned, ning, s
shunt	ed, ing, er, s
shut	ting, s
shutter	ed, ing, s
shuttle	d, ⌀ing, cock, s
shy	er, est, ly, ness

si

sick	er, est, ly, ness, -bay, -bed, -room
sicken	ed, ing, s
side	d, ⌀ing, car, light, line, -show, s
sideboard	s
sideways	
siege	s
sieve	d, ⌀ing, s
sift	ed, ing, er, s
sigh	ed, ing, s
sight* (see)	ed, ing, less, seeing, seer, s
sign	ed, ing, board, -writer, post, s
signal	led, ling, ler, man, men, s
signal-box	es
signature	-tune, s
signet* (a seal)	-ring, s
significance	
significant	ly
signify	ing
signif ied	ies

silence	d, ⌀ing, r, s
silent	ly
silhouette	d, ⌀ing, s
silk	en, worm, s
silk y	ier, iest, ily, iness
sill y	ier, iest, ily, iness, ies
silver	ed, ing, y, -paper, -plated
similar	ly
similarit y	ies
simmer	ed, ing, s
simple	r, st, ness, ton, -minded
simplicity	
simply	
simplify	ing
simplif ied	ication, ies
simultaneous	ly, ness
sin	ned, ning, ner, s
since	
sincere	r, st, ly, ness
sincerity	
sing	ing, er, -song, s
singe	d, ing, s
single	d, ⌀ing, ⌀y, -handed, s
singular	ly, s
sinister	ly
sink	ing, er, s
sip	ped, ping, per, s
siphon	ed, ing, s
sister	ly, s
sister(s)-in-law	
sit	ting, ter, s
sitting-room	s
site* (a place)	d, ⌀ing, s
situated	
situation	s
size	d, ⌀ing, s
sizzle	d, ⌀ing, s

⌀ Drop **e** before adding *ing*

*	sight	signet
	site	cygnet

sk sl

sk

skate	d, ǿing, r, board, s
skating-rink	s
skein	s
skeleton	s
sketch	ed, ing, es
sketch y	ier, iest, ily, iness
skewer	ed, ing, s
ski	-ed, -ing, er, -jump, -lift, -run, s
skid	ded, ding, s
skilful	ly, ness
skill	ed, s
skim	med, ming, mer, s
skin	ned, ning, -diving, -diver, s
skinn y	ier, iest, iness
skip	ped, ping, per, s
skipping-rope	s
skipper	ed, ing, s
skirmish	ed, ing, es
skirt	ed, ing, s
skittle	d, ǿing, r, -alley, -ball, -pin, s
skull* (head bones)	-cap, s
skulk	ed, ing, s
skunk	s
sky	ing, lark, light, -rocket, scraper
sk ied	ies

sl

slack	ed, ing, er, est, ly, ness, s
slacken	ed, ing, s
slain	
slam	med, ming, s
slang	ing, y
slant	ed, ing, wise, s
slap	ped, ping, per, dash, stick, s
slash	ed, ing, es

slate	s
slaughter	ed, ing, er, -house, s
slave	d, ǿing, r, ry, -driver, -trader, s
slay* (kill)	ing, er, s
sledge	d, ǿing, r, s
sleek	ed, ing, er, est, ly, ness, s
sleep	ing, er, less, -walking, -walker, s
sleep y	ier, iest, ily, iness
slept	
sleet	ed, ing, s
sleet y	ier, iest, iness
sleeve	d, less, -button, s
sleigh* (sledge)	ing, -bell, -horse, s
slender	ly, ness
sleuth	-hound, s
slew	
slice	d, ǿing, r, s
slick	ed, ing, er, est, ly, ness, s
slid	
slide	ǿing, r, s
slight	ed, ing, er, est, ly, ness, s
slim	med, ming, mer, mest, ly, ness, s
slime	
slim y	ier, iest, ily, iness
sling	ing, er, s
slink	ing, er, s
slink y	ier, iest, ily, iness
slip	ped, ping, knot, shod, way, s
slipper	s
slipper y	ier, iest, ily, iness
slit	ting, ter, s
slither	ed, ing, y, s
sloe* (wild plum)	-tree, s
slog	ged, ging, ger, s
slogan	s
slop	ped, ping, -basin, s
slopp y	ier, iest, ily, iness

ǿ Drop **e** before adding *ing*

*	skull	slay	sloe
	scull	sleigh	slow

sm   sn

slope	d, ∉ing, s
slot	ted, ting, -machine, -meter, s
slouch	ed, ing, es
slovenly	ier, iest, iness
slow*	ed, ing, er, est, ly, ness, s
slow-worm	s
slug	s
sluggish	ly, ness
sluice	d, ∉ing, -gate, s
slum	my, -dweller, s
slumber	ed, ing, er, s
slump	ed, ing, s
slung	
slunk	
slush	ed, ing, es
slushy	ier, iest, ily, iness
sly	er, est, ly, ness

sm

smack	ed, ing, s
small	er, est, ness
smart	ed, ing, er, est, ly, ness, s
smarten	ed, ing, s
smash	ed, ing, es
smear	ed, ing, s
smeary	ier, iest, ily, iness
smell	ed, ing, er, s
smelly	ier, iest, ily, iness
smelt or **smelled**	
smile	d, ∉ing, r, s
smirk	ed, ing, er, s
smithereens	
smock	ed, ing, s
smoke	d, ∉ing, r, -bomb, -screen, s
smoky	ier, iest, ily, iness
smooth	ed, ing, er, est, ly, ness, s

smother	ed, ing, s
smoulder	ed, ing, s
smudge	d, ∉ing, s
smudgy	ier, iest, ily, iness
smuggle	d, ∉ing, r, s
smut	ted, ting, s
smutty	ier, iest, ily, iness

sn

snack	-bar, s
snail	s
snake	d, ∉ing, ∉y, -bite, -charmer, s
snap	ped, ping, per, shot, dragon, s
snare	d, ∉ing, r, s
snarl	ed, ing, er, s
snatch	ed, ing, es
sneak	ed, ing, er, s
sneaky	ier, iest, ily, iness
sneer	ed, ing, er, s
sneeze	d, ∉ing, r, s
sniff	ed, ing, er, s
sniffle	d, ∉ing, r, s
snigger	ed, ing, er, s
snip	ped, ping, per, s
snipe	d, ∉ing, r, s
snivel	led, ling, ler, s
snob	bery, bish, bishness, s
snooker	ed
snore	d, ∉ing, r, s
snort	ed, ing, er, s
snow	ed, ing, drift, fall, flake, storm, s
snow	man, men, -plough, drop, shoe, s
snowball	ed, ing, s
snowy	ier, iest, ily, iness
snug	ger, gest, ly, ness
snuggle	d, ∉ing, s

∉ Drop e before adding *ing*

*   slow
     sloe

so

sp_a

so

soak	ed, ing, s
soap	ed, ing, -suds, -bubble, -flake, s
soapy	ier, iest, ily, iness
soar* (fly upwards)	ed, ing, s
sob	bed, bing, s
sociable	ness
social	ly, s
socialist	s
society	ies
sock	s
socket	s
soda	-bread, -fountain, -water
sodden	
sofa	s
soft	er, est, ish, ly, ness, -hearted
soften	ed, ing, er, s
soggy	ier, iest, ily, iness
soil	ed, ing, s
sold* (sell)	
solder	ed, ing, s
soldier	ed, ing, s
sole* (only)	ly
sole* (bottom of shoe, etc.)	d,* ɇing, s
sole* (fish)	s or **sole**
solemn	ity, ly, ness
solicitor	s
solid	ity, ly, s
solitary	
solo	ist, -singer, s
solution	s
solve	d, ɇing, s
some*	body, one, how, thing, where
sometime	s
somersault	ed, ing, s
son* (boy)	ny, s
song	ster, -book, -bird, -writer, s

soon	er, est
soot	
sooty	ier, iest, ily, iness
soothe	d, ɇing, s
soprano	s
sore* (painful)	r, st, ly, ness, s
sorrow	ed, ing, ful, fully, s
sorry	ier, iest, ily, iness
sort	ed, ing, er, s
soul* (spirit)	ful, fully, s
sound	ed, ing, er, est, ly, ness, s
soup	-plate, -spoon, s
sour	ed, ing, er, est, ly, ness, s
source	s
south	-east, -west, ern, erly, ward
souvenir	s
sovereign	s
sow* (scatter seed)	ed, ing, er, s
sown* (planted)	

sp

space	d, ɇing, r, s, craft, man, men
space	-capsule, ship, -station, suit, s
spacious	ly, ness
spade	ful, s
spaghetti	
span	ned, ning, s
spangle	d, ɇing, s
spaniel	s
spank	ed, ing, s
spanner	s
spare	d, ɇing, s
spark	ed, ing, s
sparkle	d, ɇing, r, s
sparrow	-hawk, s
spastic	s

ɇ Drop **e** before adding *ing*

*	soar	sold	sole	some	son	sow	sown
	sore	soled	soul	sum	sun	sew	sewn
					so		

| spe | sph | spi | | spl | spo | spr | spu | spy |

---

spat		
spawn	*ed, ing, s*	
speak	*ing, er, s*	
spear	*ed, ing, man, men, head, -gun, s*	
special	*ly, ty, ist, ity*	
specialize	*d, ǿing, s*	
specimen	*s*	
speck	*ed, ing, less, lessly, s*	
speckle	*d, ǿing, s*	
spectacle	*s*	
spectacular	*ly*	
spectator	*s*	
spectre	*s*	
sped or **speeded**		
speech	*-training, less, es*	
speed	*ed, ing, -boat, -limit, way, s*	
speed *y*	*ier, iest, ily, iness*	
spell	*ed, ing, er, bind, bound, s*	
spelt or **spelled**		
spend	*ing, er, thrift, s*	
spent		
sphere	*s*	
spider	*y, s*	
spied		
spike	*d, ǿing, s*	
spill	*ed, ing, s*	
spilt or **spilled**		
spin	*ning, ner, -dryer, s*	
spinach		
spinster	*s*	
spiral	*led, ling, ly, s*	
spire	*s*	
spirit	*ed, ing, -level, -lamp, s*	
spirt or **spurt**	*ed, ing, s*	
spit	*ting, ter, s*	
spite	*d, ǿing, s*	
spiteful	*ly, ness*	

splash	*ed, ing, es*	
splendid	*ly*	
splendour	*s*	
splint	*s*	
splinter	*ed, ing, y, s*	
split	*ting, ter, s*	
splutter	*ed, ing, er, s*	
spoil	*ed, ing, er, -sport, s*	
spoilt or **spoiled**		
spoke (speak)	*n, sman, smen*	
spoke (of wheel)	*s*	
sponge	*d, ǿing, r, -bag, -cake, s*	
spong *y*	*ier, iest, ily, iness*	
spool	*s*	
spoon	*ed, ing, ful, s*	
sport	*ed, ing, sman, smen, s*	
sport *y*	*ier, iest, ily, iness*	
spot	*ted, ting, ter, less, lessly, light, s*	
spott *y*	*ier, iest, ily, iness*	
spout	*ed, ing, s*	
sprain	*ed, ing, s*	
sprang		
sprat	*s* or **sprat**	
sprawl	*ed, ing, er, s*	
spray	*ed, ing, er, s*	
spread	*ing, er, s*	
spring	*ing, -cleaning, -board, time, s*	
spring *y*	*ier, iest, ily, iness*	
sprinkle	*d, ǿing, r, s*	
sprint	*ed, ing, er, s*	
sprout	*ed, ing, s*	
sprung		
spun		
spur	*red, ring, s*	
spurt or **spirt**	*ed, ing, s*	
spy	*ing*	
sp *ied*	*ies*	

ǿ Drop **e** before adding *ing*

sq st_a

sq

squabble	*d, ∉ing, r, s*
squad	*ron, s*
squall	*ed, ing, y, s*
squander	*ed, ing, er, s*
square	*d, ∉ing, ly, ness, -dance, root, s*
squash	*ed, ing, y, es*
squat	*ted, ting, ter, s*
squaw	*s*
squawk	*ed, ing, er, s*
squeak	*ed, ing, er, s*
squeak *y*	*ier, iest, ily, iness*
squeal	*ed, ing, er, s*
squeeze	*d, ∉ing, r, s*
squelch	*ed, ing, es*
squib	*s*
squint	*ed, ing, er, s*
squire	*d, ∉ing, s*
squirm	*ed, ing, er, s*
squirrel	*s*
squirt	*ed, ing, er, s*

st

stab	*bed, bing, ber, s*
stable	*d, ∉ing, -man, -men, -boy, s*
stack	*ed, ing, s*
stadium	*s or* **stadia**
staff	*ed, ing, -room, s*
stag	*-beetle, -horn, hound, -hunt, s*
stage	*d, ∉ing, -hand, -manager, s*
stage-coach	*es*
stagger	*ed, ing, er, s*
stain	*ed, ing, less, er, s*
stair*	*-carpet, case, -rod, way, s*
stake* (a stick; bet)	*d, ∉ing, s*
stale	*r, st, ly, ness*

stalk	*ed, ing, er, s*
stall	*ed, ing, -holder, s*
stallion	*s*
stammer	*ed, ing, er, s*
stamp	*ed, ing, -album, -collector, s*
stampede	*d, ∉ing, s*
stand	*ing, s*
standard	*-bearer, s*
star	*red, ring, less, light, lit, s*
starr *y*	*ier, iest, ily, iness*
starboard	
starfish	*es or* **starfish**
starch	*ed, ing, es*
stare* (look at)	*d, ∉ing, s*
starling	*s*
start	*ed, ing, er, s*
startle	*d, ∉ing, s*
starvation	
starve	*d, ∉ing, s*
state	*d, ∉ing, ment, s*
statel *y*	*ier, iest, ily, iness*
station	*ed, ing, -master, s*
stationary* (still)	
stationer	*s*
stationery* (paper, pens, etc.)	
statue	*tte, s*
staunch	*ed, ing, er, est, ly, ness, es*
stay	*ed, ing, er, s*
steady	*ing*
stead *ied*	*ier, iest, ily, iness, ies*
steak* (meat)	*s*
steal* (thieve)	*ing, s*
stealth	
stealth *y*	*ier, iest, ily, iness*
steam	*ed, ing, er, boat, ship, -engine, s*
steam *y*	*ier, iest, ily, iness*
steel* (metal)	*ed, ing, y, work, worker, s*

∉ Drop **e** before adding *ing*

*	stair	stake	stationary	steal
	stare	steak	stationery	steel

steep	*er, est, ly, ness*	**stool**	*-ball, s*
steeple	*chase, jack, s*	**stoop**	*ed, ing, s*
steer	*age, ed, ing, er, sman, smen, s*	**stop**	*ped, ping, page, per, s*
steering-wheel	*s*	**storage**	
stem	*med, ming, s*	**store**	*d, ∅ing, house, keeper, -room, s*
stencil	*led, ling, ler, s*	**storey*** (floor)	*s*
step	*ped, ping, -ladder, s*	**stork**	*s*
step	*father, mother, brother, sister, s*	**storm**	*ed, ing, -cloud, s*
stepping-stone	*s*	**storm** y	*ier, iest, ily, iness*
sterilize	*d, ∅ing, r, s*	**stor** y* (tale; floor)	*ies*
stern	*er, est, ly, ness*	**stout**	*er, est, ly, ness, ish, hearted*
stew	*ed, ing, er, -pot, s*	**stove**	*-pipe, s*
steward	*s*	**stow**	*ed, ing, away, s*
stewardess	*es*	**straggle**	*d, ∅ing, r, s*
stick	*ing, er, -insect, s*	**straight*** (not bent)	*er, est, ly, ness*
stick y	*ier, iest, ily, iness*	**straighten**	*ed, ing, er, s*
stickleback	*s*	**strain**	*ed, ing, er, s*
stiff	*er, est, ly, ness*	**strait*** (sea channel)	*s*
stiffen	*ed, ing, er, s*	**strand**	*ed, ing, s*
stifle	*d, ∅ing, r, s*	**strange**	*r, st, ly, ness*
stile* (steps)	*s*	**stranger**	*s*
still	*ed, ing, ness, s*	**strangle**	*d, ∅ing, hold, r, s*
sting	*ing, er, s*	**strap**	*ped, ping, less, s*
stinging-nettle	*s*	**straw**	*board, -coloured, -hat, s*
stir	*red, ring, rer, s*	**strawberr** y	*ies*
stirrup	*s*	**stray**	*ed, ing, er, s*
stitch	*ed, ing, es*	**streak**	*ed, ing, er, s*
stoat	*s*	**streak** y	*ier, iest, ily, iness*
stock	*ed, ing, ist, -car, -pot, -room, s*	**stream**	*ed, ing, lined, er, s*
stocking	*s*	**street**	*-sweeper, s*
stockade	*d, ∅ing, s*	**strength**	*s*
stoke	*d, ∅ing, r, s*	**strengthen**	*ed, ing, er, s*
stole	*n*	**strenuous**	*ly, ness*
stomach	*-ache, -pump, s*	**stretch**	*ed, ing, es*
stone	*d, ∅ing, -cold, -deaf, -mason, s*	**stretcher**	*-bearer, s*
ston y	*ier, iest, ily, iness*	**strict**	*er, est, ly, ness*
stood		**stride**	*∅ing, r, s*

∅ Drop **e** before adding *ing*

*	stile	storey	straight
	style	story	strait

stu   sty

su

strike	ø̸ing, r, s
string	ing, -bag, -vest, s
strip	ped, ping, per, -lighting, s
stripe	d, ø̸ing, s
strode	
stroke	d, ø̸ing, r, s
stroll	ed, ing, er, s
strong	er, est, ly, ish, hold, -room
struck	
structure	s
struggle	d, ø̸ing, r, s
strum	med, ming, mer, s
strung	
strut	ted, ting, ter, s
stub	bed, bing, by, s
stubborn	ly, ness
stuck	
stud	ded, ding, s
student	s
studio	s
studious	ly, ness
study	ing
stud ied	ies
stuff	ed, ing, er, s
stuff y	ier, iest, ily, iness
stumble	d, ø̸ing, r, s
stump	ed, ing, s
stump y	ier, iest, ily, iness
stun	ned, ning, ner, s
stung	
stunt	ed, ing, man, men, s
stupendous	ly, ness
stupid	ity, ly
sturd y	ier, iest, ily, iness
stutter	ed, ing, er, s
st y	ies
style* (way; fashion)	d, ø̸ing, s

	su
subject	ed, ing, s
submarine	r, s
submerge	d, ø̸ing, s
submit	ted, ting, s
subscribe	d, ø̸ing, r, s
subscription	s
subside	d, ø̸ing, s
substance	s
substantial	ly
substitute	d, ø̸ing, s
subtract	ed, ing, ion, s
suburb	s
succeed	ed, ing, s
success	es
successful	ly
succession	s
successor	s
such	like
suck	ed, ing, er, s
suction	-pump
sudden	ly, ness
suds	
suet	-pudding, y
suffer	ed, ing, er, s
sufficient	ly
suffocate	d, ø̸ing, s
suffocation	
sugar	ed, ing, y, -basin, -beet, -cane, s
suggest	ed, ing, ion, s
suicide	s
suit	ed, ing, able, ably, ability, case, s
suite* (set of furniture, rooms, etc.)	s
sulk	ed, ing, s
sulk y	ier, iest, ily, iness
sullen	ly, ness
sultana	s

ø̸ Drop **e** before adding *ing*

* style	suite
stile	sweet

SW

sum* (add up; total)	*med, ming, s*
summer	*y, -time, -house, s*
summit	*s*
summon	*ed, ing, s*
summons	*es*
sumptuous	*ly, ness*
sun*	*ned, ning, beam, light, flower, s*
sun*	*-glasses, rise, set, shine, shade, s*
sunny	*ier, iest, ily, iness*
sunbathe	*d, ∉ing, r, s*
sunburn	*ed, t*
sundae* (ice cream)	*s*
Sunday*	*-school, s*
sung	
sunk	*en*
superb	*ly*
superintend	*ed, ing, ent, s*
superior	*ity, s*
supermarket	*s*
superstition	*s*
superstitious	*ly, ness*
supervise	*d, ∉ing, s*
supervision	
supervisor	*s*
supper	*-time, s*
supple	*ness*
supply	*ing*
supplied	*ier, ies*
support	*ed, ing, er, s*
suppose	*d, ∉ing, s*
sure* (certain)	*r, st, ly, ness, -footed*
surf* (sea foam)	*ing, -board, -riding*
surface	*d, ∉ing, s*
surge	*d, ∉ing, s*
surgeon	*s*
surgery	*ies*
surname	*s*

surplice* (gown)	*s*
surplus* (left over)	*es*
surprise	*d, ∉ing, s*
surrender	*ed, ing, s*
surround	*ed, ing, s*
survey	*ed, ing, or, s*
survival	
survive	*d, ∉ing, s*
survivor	*s*
suspect	*ed, ing, s*
suspend	*ed, ing, er, s*
suspense	
suspicion	*s*
suspicious	*ly, ness*
sustain	*ed, ing, s*

SW

swagger	*ed, ing, er, -cane, -coat, -stick, s*
swallow	*ed, ing, er, s*
swam	
swamp	*ed, ing, s*
swampy	*ier, iest, ily, iness*
swan	*s*
swap or **swop**	*ped, ping, per, s*
swarm	*ed, ing, s*
swarthy	*ier, iest, ily, iness*
sway	*ed, ing, s*
swear	*ing, er, -word, s*
sweat	*ed, ing, y, er, -band, -shirt, -suit, s*
swede	*s*
sweep	*ing, er, stake, s*
swept	
sweet*	*er, est, ish, ly, ness, heart, -pea, s*
sweeten	*ed, ing, er, s*
swell	*ed, ing, s*
swelter	*ed, ing, s*

∉ Drop **e** before adding *ing*

*	sum	sun	sundae	sure	surf	surplice	sweet
	some	son	Sunday	shore	serf	surplus	suite

sy   ta

swept	
swerve	d, ɇing, s
swift	er, est, ly, ness, s
swill	ed, ing, s
swim	mer, suit, s
swimming	-bath, -pool
swindle	d, ɇing, r, s
swine	herd. **swine**
swing	ing, er, s
swipe	d, ɇing, r, s
swirl	ed, ing, s
swish	ed, ing, es
switch	ed, ing, es
swivel	led, ling, s
swollen	
swoon	ed, ing, s
swoop	ed, ing, s
swop or **swap**	ped, ping, per, s
sword	sman, smen, -dance, s
swordfish	es or **swordfish**
swore	
sworn	
swum	
swung	

sy

sycamore	-tree, s
sympathetic	ally
sympathize	d, ɇing, r, s
sympathy	ies
symphony	ies
symptom	s
synagogue	s
syringe	d, ɇing, s
syrup	y
system	atic, atically, s

ta

tabby-cat	s
table	-tennis, -cloth, -mat, s
table-spoon	ful, s
tableau	x or s
tablet	s
tack	ed, ing, s
tackle	d, ɇing, r, s
tact	ful, fully, less, lessly
tactics	
tadpole	s
tag	ged, ging, s
tail*	ed, ing, -end, -lamp, -light, -spin, s
tailor	ed, ing, -made, s
take	n, ɇing, r, -away, -off, s
talcum powder	
tale* (story)	-bearer, -teller, s
talent	ed, s
talk	ative, ed, ing, er, s
tall	er, est, ish, ness
tambourine	s
tame	d, ɇing, r, st, ly, ness, s
tamper	ed, ing, er, s
tan	ned, ning, ner, s
tandem	s
tangerine	s
tangle	d, ɇing, s
tango	ed, ing, s
tank	er, ful, -trap, s
tankard	s
tantalize	d, ɇing, s
tantrum	s
tap	ped, ping, per, -dance, -dancing, s
tape	d, ɇing, s
tape	-measure, -recorder, -recording, s
tapestry	ies
tapioca	

ɇ Drop **e** before adding *ing*

* tail
    tale

te

tar	red, ring, ry, s
tarantula	s
tare* (weed)	s
target	s
tarnish	ed, ing, es
tarpaulin	s
tart	let, s
tartan	s
task	ed, ing, master, s
tassel	s
taste	d, ɇing, r, s
tasteful	ly, ness
tasteless	ly, ness
tatter	ed, ing, s
tattoo	ed, ing, er, ist, -mark, s
taught* (teach)	
taunt	ed, ing, er, s
taut* (tight)	er, est, ly, ness
tavern	s
tax	ation, ed, ing, es
taxi	-cab, -driver, -rank, s

te

tea*	cake, -cloth, cup, pot, -service, s
tea*	-set, -things, -time, -table, -tray, s
tea-cos y	ies
tea-leaf	-leaves
tea-part y	ies
tea-spoon	ful, s
teach	ing, ings, es
teacher	s
teak	
team* (side; number)	-work, s
tear* (pull apart)	ing, s
tear	-gas, -drop, s
tearful	ly, ness

tease	d, ɇing, r, s
technical	ly
technician	s
Teddy bear	s
tedious	ly, ness
tee* (golf)	d, ing, -shot, s
tee-shirt or **T-shirt**	s
teem* (pour; swarm)	ed, ing, s
teenage	d, -boy, -girl
teenager	s
teeth	
telegram	s
telegraph	ed, ing, -line, -pole, -wire, s
telephone	d, ɇing, s
telescope	d, ɇing, s
televise	d, ɇing, s
television	s
tell	ing, er, -tale, s
temper	ed, ing, s
temperature	s
temple	s
temporar y	ily
tempt	ation, ed, ing, er, s
tend	ed, ing, s
tender	-hearted, ly, ness
tenement	s
tennis	-ball, -court, -racket
tenor	s
tense	d, ɇing, r, st, ly, ness, s
tent	-peg, -pole, -rope, s
tentacle	s
tepid	ly, ness
term	ly, ed, ing, s
terminus	es or **termini**
terrace	d, ɇing, -house, s
terrible	ness
terribly	

ɇ Drop **e** before adding ing

*	tare	taught	tea	team
	tear	taut	tee	teem

th

terrier	*s*
terrific	*ally*
terrify	*ing*
terrif *ied*	*ies*
territorial	*s*
territor *y*	*ies*
terror	*ism, ist, -stricken, s*
terrorize	*d, ∉ing, s*
test	*ed, ing, -paper, -piece, -tube, s*
testament	*s*
testimonial	*s*
tetanus	
tether	*ed, ing, s*
text	*-book, s*
textile	*s*

th

than	
thank	*ed, ing, -offering, s*
thankful	*ly, ness*
thankless	*ly, ness*
that	
that's (that is)	
thatch	*ed, ing, es*
thaw	*ed, ing, s*
theatre	*-ticket, s*
theatrical	*ly, s*
theft	*s*
their* (belonging to them)	
theirs* (belonging to them)	
them	*selves*
then	
theor *y*	*ies*
there* (in that place)	*abouts, after*
therefore	
there's* (there is)	

thermometer	*s*
thermos flask	*s*
these	
they	
they'll (they will; they shall)	
they're* (they are)	
they've (they have)	
thick	*er, est, ly, ness, ish, -skinned*
thicken	*ed, ing, er, s*
thicket	*s*
thief	**thieves**
thieve	*d, ∉ing, s*
thimble	*ful, s*
thin	*ned, ning, ner, nest, ly, ness, s*
thing	*s*
think	*ing, er, s*
thirst	*ed, ing, s*
thirst *y*	*ier, iest, ily, iness*
this	
thistle	*s*
thorn	*s*
thorn *y*	*ier, iest, ily, iness*
thorough	*ly, ness, bred, fare*
those	
though	
thought	*-reader, s*
thoughtful	*ly, ness*
thoughtless	*ly, ness*
thrash	*ed, ing, ings, es*
thread	*ed, ing, bare, er, s*
threat	*s*
threaten	*ed, ing, s*
thresh	*ed, ing, es*
threw* (throw)	
thrift	*less*
thrift *y*	*ier, iest, ily, iness*
thrill	*ed, ing, er, s*

∉ Drop **e** before adding *ing*

	their	theirs		threw
*	there	there's		through
	they're			

ti ⎪ to

thrive	*d, ∉ing, s*
throat	*s*
throb	*bed, bing, s*
throne* (king's seat)	*s*
throng	*ed, ing, s*
throttle	*d, ∉ing, s*
through* (from end to end)	*out*
throw	*ing, er, n,* s*
thrush	*es*
thrust	*ing, s*
thud	*ded, ding, s*
thug	*s*
thumb	*ed, ing, -mark, -nail, screw, s*
thump	*ed, ing, er, s*
thunder	*ed, ing, y, bolt, clap, storm, s*
Thursday	*s*

ti

tiara	*s*
tick	*ed, ing, s*
ticket	*-collector, -office, s*
tickle	*d, ∉ing, r, s*
ticklish	*ly, ness*
tide* (sea)	*-mark, s*
tidings	
tidy	*ing*
tid *ied*	*ier, iest, ily, iness, ies*
tie	*d,* -clip, -pin, s*
tying	
tiger	*-cat, -moth, s*
tigress	*es*
tight	*er, est, ly, ness, -rope, s*
tighten	*ed, ing, er, s*
tile	*d, ∉ing, r, s*
till	*ed, ing, er, s*
till or **until**	

tilt	*ed, ing, er, s*
timber	*ed, -mill, -yard, s*
time	*d, ∉ing, r, ly, less, -bomb, table, s*
timid	*ity, ly, ness*
tin	*ned, ning, ny, -opener, foil, -tack, s*
tinge	*d, ∉ing, s*
tingle	*d, ∉ing, s*
tinker	*ed, ing, s*
tinkle	*d, ∉ing, s*
tinsel	*led, ling, ly*
tint	*ed, ing, s*
tin *y*	*ier, iest, ily, iness*
tip	*ped, ping, per, ster, s*
tiptoe	*d, ing, s*
tire* (weary)	*d, ∉ing, some, s*
tired	*ness*
tireless	*ly, ness*
tissue	*-paper, s*
title	*d, s*
titter	*ed, ing, s*

to

to* (towards)	
toad	*-in-the-hole, s*
toadstool	*s*
to and fro	
toast	*ed, ing, er, -rack, s*
tobacco	*nist, -pipe, -plant, s*
toboggan	*ed, ing, er, s*
today or **to-day**	
toddle	*d, ∉ing, r, s*
toe*	*d, ing, -cap, -hold, -nail, s*
toffee	*-apple, s*
together	*ness*
toil	*ed, ing, er, s*
toilet	*-paper, -roll, -soap, s*

*∉ Drop **e** before adding ing*

* throne	through	tide	tire	toe	to
thrown	threw	tied	tyre	tow	too
					two (2)

token	s	**toss**	ed, ing, es	
told		**total**	led, ling, ly, s	
tolerate	d, ǿing, s	**totter**	ed, ing, y, er, s	
toll ed, ing, -bridge, -gate, s		**touch**	ed, ing, y, es	
tomahawk	s	**tough**	er, est, ly, ness, s	
tomato	es	**toughen**	ed, ing, s	
tomb	stone, s	**tour**	ed, ing, ist, s	
tomcat	s	**tournament**	s	
tomorrow or **to-morrow**	s	**tousle**	d, ǿing, s	
tomtit	s	**tow*** (pull)	ed, ing, -line, -path, -rope, s	
ton or **tonne** (metric)	s	**towards** or **toward**		
tone	d, ǿing, -deaf, s	**towel**	led, ling, -rail, s	
tongs		**tower**	ed, ing, -block, s	
tongue	-tied, -twister, s	**town**	-council, -crier, -hall, s	
tonic	s	**toy**	ed, ing, shop, s	
tonight or **to-night**				
tonsil	s			
tonsillitis			**tr**	
too* (more than enough; also)		**trace**	d, ǿing, r, s	
took		**tracing-paper**		
tool -bag, -chest, -shed, s		**track**	ed, ing, er, suit, s	
tooth ache, paste, powder, less, **teeth**		**tractor**	s	
tooth-brush	es	**trade** d, ǿing, mark, sman, smen, r, s		
top ped, ping, per, knot, -heavy, -hat, s		**traffic**	-sign, -signal, -lights	
topic	s	**traged** y	ies	
topple	d, ǿing, s	**tragic**	ally	
topsy-turvy		**trail**	ed, ing, er, s	
torch	es	**train**	ed, ing, er, s	
tore		**traitor**	ous, ously, s	
torment	ed, ing, or, s	**tramp**	ed, ing, er, s	
torn		**trample**	d, ǿing, r, s	
tornado	es	**trampoline**	s	
torpedo	ed, ing, es	**transfer**	red, ring, able, s	
torrent	s	**transform**	ed, ing, ation, s	
torrential	ly	**transistor**	-radio, s	
tortoise	-shell, s	**translate**	d, ǿing, s	
torture d, ǿing, r, -chamber, s		**translation**	s	

ǿ Drop **e** before adding *ing*

*   too   tow
      to   toe
      two (2)

tre   tri   tro   tru   try

transparent	ly, ness
transport	ed, ing, er, ation, able, s
trap	ped, ping, per, -door, s
trapeze	s
travel	led, ling, ler, s
trawl	ed, ing, er, s
tray	-cloth, ful, s
treacherous	ly, ness
treacher y	ies
treacle	
tread	ing, s
treason	able
treasure	d, ∅ing, r, -chest, -hunt, s
treat	ed, ing, ment, s
treble	d, ∅ing, s
tree	-stump, -top, -trunk, s
trek	ked, king, ker, s
trellis	-work
tremble	d, ∅ing, s
tremendous	ly, ness
trench	es
trespass	ed, ing, es
trespasser	s
trestle	-table, s
trial	s
triangle	s
tribe	sman, smen, s
tributar y	ies
trick	ed, ing, ery, ster, s
trick y	ier, iest, ily, iness
trickle	d, ∅ing, s
tricycle	d, ∅ing, s
tried	
trier	s
tries	
trifle	d, ∅ing, s
trigger	ed, ing, s

trim	med, ming, mer, mest, ly, ness, s
trinket	s
trio	s
trip	ped, ping, per, s
triple	d, ∅ing, s
triplet	s
tripod	s
triumph	ed, ing, ant, antly, s
trod	den
trolley	s
trombone	∅ist, s
troop* (of scouts, soldiers)	ed, ing, er, s
troph y	ies
tropic	al, ally, s
trot	ted, ting, ter, s
trouble	d, ∅ing, some, -maker, s
trough	s
troupe* (of entertainers)	r, s
trousers	
trousseau	x or s
trout	trout
trowel	s
truant	s
truck	-load, s
trudge	d, ∅ing, s
true	r, st, ness
truly	
trumpet	ed, ing, er, -call, s
truncheon	s
trunk	s
truss	ed, ing, es
trust	ed, ing, worthy, s
trust y	ier, iest, ily, iness
truth	s
truthful	ly, ness
try	ing
tr ied	ier, ies

∅ Drop **e** before adding *ing*

* troop
  troupe

tu   tw   ty   ug   um

tu	
tuba	s
tubby	ier, iest, iness
tube	∉ing, less, -train, s
tuck	ed, ing, -shop, s
Tudor	s
Tuesday	s
tuft	s
tug	ged, ging, ger, boat, s
tug-of-war	
tuition	
tulip	s
tumble	d, ∉ing, r, down, -dryer, s
tumbler	ful, s
tumult	s
tumultuous	ly, ness
tundra	s
tune	d, ∉ing, r, s
tuneful	ly, ness
tuneless	ly, ness
tunic	s
tunnel	led, ling, ler, s
turban	s
turbine	s
turf	ed, ing, s or **turves**
turkey	cock, s
Turkish delight	
turmoil	
turn	ed, ing, er, over, stile, table, s
turnip	s
turpentine	
turquoise	s
turret	ed, s
turtle	-neck, -shell, -soup, -dove, ·s
tusk	s
tussle	d, ∉ing, s
tutor	ial, s

tw	
twang	ed, ing, s
tweed	s
tweezers	
twice	
twiddle	d, ∉ing, r, s
twig	s
twilight	
twin	ned, ning, -brother, -sister, s
twine	d, ∉ing, s
twinge	d, ∉ing, s
twinkle	d, ∉ing, s
twirl	ed, ing, s
twist	ed, ing, er, s
twisty	ier, iest, ily, iness
twitch	ed, ing, es
twitter	ed, ing, s

ty	
tying	
type	d, ∉ing, written, writing, writer, s
typist	s
typhoon	s
typical	ly, ness
tyrannize	d, ∉ing, s
tyrant	s
tyre* (wheel cover)·	s

ug	
ugly	ier, iest, ily, iness

um	
umbrella	-stand, s
umpire	d, ∉ing, s

∉ Drop **e** before adding *ing*

* tyre
  tire

un

un		undertake	n, ǿing, r, s
unable		undertook	
unafraid		undid	
unaided		undo	ing
unarm	ed, ing, s	undone	
unattractive	ly, ness	undoubted	ly
unavoidabl e	y	undress	ed, ing, es
unaware	s	uneas y	ier, iest, ily, iness
unbalance	d, ǿing, s	unemploy ed	ment
unbearabl e	y	uneven	ly, ness
unbeaten		unexpected	ly, ness
unbolt	ed, ing, s	unexplored	
unbuckle	d, ǿing, s	unfair	ly, ness
unbutton	ed, ing, s	unfasten	ed, ing, s
uncann y	ily, iness	unfinished	
uncertain	ly, ty	unfit	ted, ting, s
uncivilized		unfold	ed, ing, s
uncle	s	unfortunate	ly
unclean	liness	unfriendl y	iness
uncomfortable	ness	unfurnished	
uncommon	ly, ness	ungrateful	ly, ness
unconscious	ly, ness	unguarded	ly, ness
uncork	ed, ing, s	unhapp y	ier, iest, ily, iness
uncover	ed, ing, s	unharmed	
uncurl	ed, ing, s	unhealth y	ier, iest, ily, iness
undamaged		unhurt	
undecided	ly	uniform	ed, s
under	clothes, clothing, wear	unimportant	
under	go, going, goes, gone, went	uninhabited	
undercurrent	s	uninjured	
underground		uninteresting	
undergrowth		Union Jack	s
underneath		unite	d, ǿing, s
understand	able, ing, s	universe	
understood		universit y	ies
understudy	ing	unjust	ly, ness
understud ied	ies	unkind	er, est, ly, ness

ǿ Drop **e** before adding *ing*

unknown	
unlawful	*ly, ness*
unless	
unlike	*ness*
unlikel y	*ier, iest, ihood*
unload	*ed, ing, s*
unlock	*ed, ing, s*
unluck y	*ier, iest, ily, iness*
unmistakabl e	*y*
unnecessar y	*ily*
unoccupied	
unpack	*ed, ing, s*
unpleasant	*ly, ness*
unpopular	*ity, ly*
unravel	*led, ling, s*
unreasonabl e	*y*
unreliable	*ness*
unroll	*ed, ing, s*
unsaddle	*d, ȼing, s*
unsafe	*r, st, ly, ness*
unscrew	*ed, ing, s*
unselfish	*ly, ness*
unstead y	*ier, iest, ily, iness*
unsuitable	
untangle	*d, ȼing, s*
untid y	*ier, iest, ily, iness*
untie	*d, s*
untying	
until or **till**	
untrue	
unusual	*ly, ness*
unveil	*ed, ing, s*
unwelcome	
unwell	
unwilling	*ly, ness*
unwise	*ly*
unwrap	*ped, ping, s*

up	
upbringing	
upheaval	*s*
upholster	*ed, ing, er, s*
upholster y	*ies*
upkeep	
upon	
upper	*most, -cut, s*
upright	*ly, ness, s*
uprising	*s*
uproar	*s*
uproot	*ed, ing, s*
upset	*ting, s*
upside-down	
upstairs	
upstream	
upturn	*ed, ing, s*
upward	*ly, s*

ur	
uranium	
urban	
urchin	*s*
urge	*d, ȼing, s*
urgenc y	*ies*
urgent	*ly*
urn* (vase; tea-urn)	*s*

us	
use	*d, ȼing, r, s*
useful	*ly, ness*
useless	*ly, ness*
usher	*ed, ing, s*
usherette	*s*
usual	*ly, ness*

ȼ Drop **e** before adding *ing*

* urn
earn

ut va   ve

ut

utensil	s
utmost	
utter	ed, ing, ance, s
utter	ly, most, ness

va

vacanc y	ies
vacant	ly
vacate	d, ǿing, s
vacation	s
vaccinate	d, ǿing, s
vacuum	-cleaner, -flask, s
vague	r, st, ly, ness
vain* (proud)	er, est, ly
vale* (valley)	s
valentine	s
valiant	ly
valley	s
valuable	s
value	d, ǿing, less, r, s
valve	s
vane* (weathercock)	s
vanilla	
vanish	ed, ing, es
vanit y	ies
vanquish	ed, ing, es
variet y	ies
various	ly, ness
varnish	ed, ing, es
vary	ing
var ied	ies
vase	s
vaseline	
vast	er, est, ly, ness
vault	ed, ing, er, s

ve

veal	
vegetable	s
vegetarian	s
vegetation	
vehicle	s
veil* (a covering)	ed, ing, s
vein* (blood-vessel)	ed, ing, s
velvet	y, s
vengeance	
venison	
vent	ed, ing, -hole, s
ventilate	d, ǿing, s
ventilation	
ventilator	s
ventriloquist	s
venture	d, ǿing, some, s
veranda(h)	s
verb	al, ally, s
verdict	s
verge	d, ǿing, s
verger	s
vermilion	s
vermin	ous, ously
verse	s
version	s
versus	
vertical	ly
very	
vessel	s
vest	s
vestibule	s
vestr y	ies
vet	ted, ting, s
veteran	s
veterinar y	ies
vex	ed, ing, es, ation, atious

ǿ Drop e before adding ing

*	vain	vale
	vane	veil
	vein	

vi   vo   vu   wa

vi	
viaduct	s
vibrate	d, ɇing, s
vibration	s
vicar	age, s
vice	-admiral, -captain, s
vicious	ly, ness
victim	s
victor	s
victorious	ly, ness
victor y	ies
victual	led, ling, ler, s
videotape	d, ɇing, s
view	ed, ing, er, point, s
vigorous	ly, ness
vigour	
viking	s
vile	r, st, ly, ness
villa	s
village	r, s
villain* (scoundrel)	ous, ously, s
villein* (serf)	s
vine	yard, s
vinegar	y
violence	
violent	ly
violet	s
violin	ist, s
virtue	s
visibl e	y
visibility	
vision	s
visit	ed, ing, or, s
vital	ity, ly
vivarium	s or vivaria
vivid	ly, ness
vixen	s

vo	
vocabular y	ies
vocalist	s
voice	d, ɇing, s
volcano	es
vole	s
volley	ēd, ing, -ball, s
volt	age, s
volume	s
voluntar y	ily
volunteer	ed, ing, s
vomit	ed, ing, s
vote	d, ɇing, r, s
vouch	ed, ing, es
voucher	s
vow	ed, ing, s
vowel	s
voyage	d, ɇing, r, s

vu	
vulgar	ity, ly
vulnerable	ness
vulture	s

wa	
waddle	d, ɇing, r, s
wade	d, ɇing, r, s
wafer	s
waft	ed, ing, er, s
wag	ged, ging, ger, s
wage	d, ɇing, r, -earner, s
waggle	d, ɇing, r, s
wagon or waggon	er, -load, s
waif	s
wail	ed, ing, er, s

ɇ Drop e before adding ing

```
       villain
  *
       villein
```

we

waist* (of body)	coat, s
wait* (stay; serve)	ed, ing, s
waiter	s
waitress	es
waiting-room	s
wake	d, ɇing, r, s
waken	ed, ing, er, s
walk	ed, ing, er, s
walking-stick	s
wall	ed, ing, chart, flower, paper, s
wallet	s
wallow	ed, ing, er, s
walnut	-tree, s
walrus	es
waltz	ed, ing, es
wand	s
wander	ed, ing, er, s
wangle	d, ɇing, r, s
want	ed, ing, s
war*	-dance, -paint, -path, ship, s
war-cry	ies
warrior	s
warble	d, ɇing, r, s
ward	ed, ing, en, er, s
wardrobe	s
ware* (goods)	house, s
warm	th, ed, ing, er, est, ish, ly, s
warn* (be careful)	ed, ing, er, s
warp	ed, ing, s
warrant	ed, ing, s
warren	s
wart	s
wary	ier, iest, ily, iness
wash	able, ed, ing, es
washer	s
wasn't (was not)	
wasp	s

waste*	d, ɇing, land, -bin, -paper, -pipe, s
wasteful	ly, ness
watch	ed, ing, man, men, es
watchful	ly, ness
water	ed, ing, -colour, cress, fall, proof, s
water-lily	ies
watery	ier, iest, ily, iness
wave	d, ɇing, s
waver	ed, ing, er, s
wavy	ier, iest, ily, iness
wax	ed, ing, en, es, works
waxy	ier, iest, ily, iness
way* (direction; manner; road)	lay, side, s

we

weak* (not strong)	er, est, ly, ness, -kneed
weaken	ed, ing, s
weakling	s
wealth	
wealthy	ier, iest, ily, iness
weapon	s
wear* (dressed in)	ing, er, s
weary	ing
wearied	ier, iest, ily, iness, ies
weasel	s
weather*	ed, ing, cock, -forecast, -vane, s
weave	d, ɇing, r, s
we'd (we had; we should; we would)	
wed	ded, ding, s
wedding	-cake, -card, -day, -ring, -bell, s
wedding-dress	es
wedge	d, ɇing, s
Wednesday	s
weed	ed, ing, er, -killer, s
weedy	ier, iest, iness
week* (seven days)	-day, -end, s

ɇ Drop **e** before adding *ing*

waist	wait	war	ware	warn	way	weak	weather
waste	weight	wore	wear	worn	weigh	week	whether

wh

weekly	*ies*
weep	*ing, y, er, s*
wept	
weigh* (measure heaviness)	*ed, ing, s*
weight* (heaviness)	*ed, ing, -lifter, s*
weighty	*ier, iest, ily, iness*
weir	*s*
weird	*er, est, ly, ness*
welcome	*d, ǿing, s*
weld	*ed, ing, er, s*
welfare	
well	*-behaved, -bred, -wisher, s*
we'll (we shall; we will)	
wellington boot	*s*
went	
wept	
we're (we are)	
were	
weren't (were not)	
west	*ern, erly, ward, wards*
wet	*ted, ting, ter, test, ly, ness, s*
we've (we have)	

wh

whack	*ed, ing, s*
whale	*ǿing, r, bone, -boat, s*
wharf	*s* or **wharves**
what	*ever, soever*
what's (what is)	
wheat	*-field, -flour, germ, s*
wheedle	*d, ǿing, r, s*
wheel	*ed, ing, er, barrow, -chair, s*
wheeze	*d, ǿing, s*
whelk	*s*
when	*ever*
whence	

where	*abouts, as, by, fore, upon*
wherever	
whether* (if)	
which* (what one? who?)	*ever*
whiff	*ed, ing, s*
while	*d, ǿing, s*
whilst	
whimper	*ed, ing, er, s*
whine* (cry; wail)	*d, ǿing, r, s*
whip	*ped, ping, per, s*
whippet	*s*
whirl	*ed, ing, igig, pool, wind, s*
whisk	*ed, ing, er, s*
whisker	*ed, y, s*
whisky	*ies*
whisper	*ed, ing, er, s*
whist	*-drive*
whistle	*d, ǿing, r, s*
white	*r, st, ly, ness, s*
whiten	*ed, ing, er, s*
whitewash	*ed, ing, es*
whiting	*s* or **whiting**
Whit Sunday	*s*
Whitsun	*tide*
whiz *zes* or **whizz**	*ed, ing, es*
who	*ever*
who'd (who had; who would)	
who'll (who will; who shall)	
who're (who are)	
who's* (who is)	
whom	*soever*
whole* (all; complete)	*sale, some*
wholly* (completely)	
whoop	*ed, ing, s*
whortleberry	*ies*
whose* (belonging to whom)	
why	

ǿ Drop **e** before adding *ing*

*	weigh	weight	whether	which	whine	who's	whole	wholly
	way	wait	weather	witch	wine	whose	hole	holy

wi   wo

wi	
wicked	er, est, ly, ness
wicker	work
wicket	-keeper, s
wide	r, st, ly, spread, s
widen	ed, ing, er, s
width	s
widow	ed, ing, er, s
wield	ed, ing, er, s
wife	ly, **wives**
wiggle	d, ẟing, r, s
wigwam	s
wild	er, est, ly, ness, life, fowl, fire, s
wilderness	es
wilful	ly, ness
will	ed, ing, -power, s
willing	ly, ness
willow	-herb, -tree, -warbler, s
wil y	ier, iest, ily, iness
win	ning, ner, s
wince	d, ẟing, s
wind (turn; twist)	ing, er, s
wind	ed, ing, -chart, fall, mill, ward, s
wind y	ier, iest, ily, iness
window	-cleaner, -ledge, -pane, -sill, s
windscreen	-wiper, s
wine* (a drink)	d, ẟing, -bottle, cask, s
wing	ed, ing, er, -span, s
wink	ed, ing, er, s
winkle	d, ẟing, s
winter	ed, ing, -time, s
wintr y	ier, iest, ily, iness
wipe	d, ẟing, r, s
wire	d, ẟing, -netting, -rope, -cutter, s
wireless	ed, ing, es
wir y	ier, iest, ily, iness
wisdom	-tooth, -teeth

wo	
wise	r, st, ly
wish	ed, ing, es
wishful	ly, ness
wistful	ly, ness
wit	ted, less, s
witt y	ier, iest, ily, iness
witch* (old woman)	es, craft, -hunt
with	in, out
withdraw	al, ing, n, s
withdrew	
wither	ed, ing, s
withstand	ing, s
withstood	
witness	ed, ing, -box, es
wizard	ry, s
wizened	
wo	
wobble	d, ẟing, r, s
woe	begone, s
woeful	ly, ness
woke	n
wolf	-cub, -pack, **wolves**
woman	hood, ly, **women**
won* (win)	
wonder	ed, ing, ment, land, s
wonderful	ly, ness
won't (will not)	
wood*	ed, man, men, -cutter, land, s
wooden	ly, ness
wood-louse	-lice
woodpecker	s
woodwork	
wool	s
woollen	s
wooll y	ier, iest, iness, ies

ẟ Drop **e** before adding *ing*

*
wine	witch	won	wood
whine	which	one (1)	would

wr   x ya ye

word	*ed, ing, s*
wore* (wear)	
work	*ed, ing, man, men, shop, er, s*
world	*-famous, -wide, s*
worm	*ed, ing, y, eaten, -cast, -hole, s*
worn* (wear)	*-out*
worry	*ing*
worr*ied*	*ier, ies, isome*
worse	
worsen	*' ed, ing, s*
worst	
worship	*ped, ping, per, s*
worth	*while*
worthless	*ly, ness*
worth *y*	*ier, iest, ily, iness, ies*
would* (past of will)	
wouldn't (would not)	
wound (turned; twisted)	
wound (injure)	*ed, ing, s*
wove	*n*

wr

wrangle	*d, ęing, r, s*
wrap* (cover)	*ped, ping, per, s*
wrath	*ful, fully*
wreath	*s*
wreck	*age, ed, ing, er, s*
wren	*s*
wrench	*ed, ing, es*
wrestle	*d, ęing, r, s*
wretch	*es*
wretched	*ly, ness*
wriggle	*d, ęing, r, s*
wring* (twist)	*ing, er, s*
wrinkle	*d, ęing, r, s*
wrist	*let, band, s*

write* (form letters)	*r, s*
writing	*-case, -desk, -paper, -table, s*
written	
writhe	*d, ęing, s*
wrong	*ed, ing, ful, ly, ness, s*
wrote	
wrung* (twisted)	
wry	*er, est, ly, ness*

x

X-ray	*ed, ing, s*
xylophone	*s*

ya

yacht	*ing, sman, smen, -club, s*
yak	*s*
yap	*ped, ping, per, s*
yard	*age, stick, s*
yarn	*ed, ing, s*
yawn	*ed, ing, s*

ye

year	*ly, ling, s*
yearn	*ed, ing, s*
yeast	*y*
yell	*ed, ing, er, s*
yellow	*er, est, ness, ish, y, s*
yelp	*ed, ing, er, s*
yeo *man*	*men*
yes	*es*
yesterday	*s*
yet	
yeti	*s*
yew*	*-tree, s*

ę Drop **e** before adding *ing*

*	wore	worn	would	wrap	wring	write	wrung	yew
	war	warn	wood	rap	ring	right	rung	you
								ewe

yi

yield	*ed, ing, s*

yo

yodel	*led, ling, ler, s*
yoga	
yog(h)urt	
yoke* (wooden bar; join)	*d, ₑing, s*
yokel	*s*
yolk* (of egg)	*s*
yonder	
Yorkshire pudding	*s*
you* (person)	
you'd (you had; you would)	
you'll (you will)	
you're (you are)	
you've (you have)	
young	*er, est, ish*
youngster	*s*
your	
yours	
your *self*	*selves*
youth	*-club, s*
youthful	*ly, ness*
yowl	*ed, ing, er, s*

yu

yule	*-log, tide, s*

ze

zeal	
zealous	*ly*
zebra	*s*
zebu	*s*
zephyr	*s*
zero	*s*
zest	*ful, fully*

zi

zigzag	*ged, ging, s*
zinc	
zip	*ped, ping, per, -fastener, s*
zither	*s*

zo

zodiac	
zone	*d, ₑing, s*
zoo	*s*
zoological garden	*s*
zoologist	*s*
zoology	
zoom	*ed, ing, s*

zu

Zulu	*s*

ₑ Drop **e** before adding *ing*

*	yoke	you
	yolk	yew
		ewe

Boys' Names

A
Aaron
Adam
Adrian
Alan
Alexander
Alistair
Alfred
Allan
Andrew
Angus
Anthony
Antony
Arthur
Ashley

B
Barry
Benjamin
Bernard
Brendan
Brian
Bryan
Bruce

C
Calvin
Carl
Cedric
Charles
Christian
Christopher
Clifford
Clive
Colin
Courtenay
Craig

D
Dale
Damian
Daniel
Darren
David
Dean
Dennis
Derek
Dominic
Donald
Duncan
Dylan

E
Edmund
Edward
Eric

F
Francis
Frank
Frederick

G
Gareth
Gary
Gavin
Geoffrey
George
Giles
Glen(n)
Glyn
Gordon
Graham
Gregory
Guy

H
Henry
Howard
Hugh

I
Ian
Ivan

J
James
Jamie
Jason
Jeffrey
Jeremy
Jocelyn
John
Jonathan
Joseph
Julian
Justin

K
Karl
Keith
Kenneth
Kevin

L
Lance
Laurence
Lawrence
Lee
Leon
Leonard
Leslie
Luke

M
Malcolm
Marc
Marcus
Mark
Martin
Martyn
Matthew
Maurice
Melvin
Mervyn
Michael
Miles

N
Nathan
Nathaniel
Neil
Neville
Nicholas
Nigel
Noel
Norman

O
Oliver
Owen

P
Patrick
Paul
Peter
Philip
Piers

Q
Quentin

R
Ralph
Randolph
Raymond
Reginald
Rex
Richard
Robert
Robin
Roderick
Rodney
Roger
Roland
Rolf
Ronald
Roy
Royston
Rufus
Rupert
Russell
Ryan

S
Samuel
Scott
Sebastian
Seán
Shane
Shaun
Sidney
Simon
Spencer
Stanley
Stephen
Steven
Stewart
Stuart

T
Terence
Terry
Thomas
Timothy
Tony
Trevor
Tristram

V
Vernon
Victor
Vincent
Vivian

W
Wallace
Walter
Warren
Wayne
Wilfred
William
Winston

Girls' Names

A
Abigail
Adele
Adrienne
Aileen
Alexandra
Alexis
Alice
Alison
Amanda
Amelia
Amy
Andrea
Angela
Anita
Ann(e)
Anna
Annabel
Annabella
Annette
Anthea
Antonia
April
Audra
Audrey
Averil

B
Barbara
Belinda
Beryl
Betty
Beverley
Blanche
Brenda
Bridget
Bryony

C
Cara
Carla
Carol(e)
Caroline
Carolyn
Carrie
Catherine
Cecilia
Celia
Charlotte
Charmaine
Cheryl
Chloe
Christine
Claire
Clare
Claudia
Colette
Corinne

D
Danielle
Daphne
Dawn
Debbie
Deborah
Debra
Deirdre
Delia
Della
Denise
Diana
Diane
Dionne
Donna
Dorothy

E
Eileen
Elaine
Eleanor
Elizabeth
Ellen
Emily
Emma
Enid
Erica
Esmé(e)
Estelle
Ester
Eveline
Evelyn

F
Fay(e)
Felicity
Fiona
Fleur
Frances

G
Gabrielle
Gail
Gayle
Gaynor
Gemma
Georgina
Geraldine
Germaine
Gillian
Gina
Glenda
Glynis
Gwyneth

H
Hannah
Hayley
Hazel
Heather
Heidi
Helen
Hilary
Holly

I
Irene
Isabel

J
Jacqueline
Jane
Janet
Janice
Janine
Jayne
Jean
Jeanette
Jennifer
Jessica
Jill
Joan
Joanna
Joanne
Johanna
Josephine
Joy
Judith
Julia
Julie
June
Justine

K

Karen
Kate
Katharine
Katherine
Kathleen
Kathryn
Katrina
Kay
Keeley
Kelly
Kerry
Kimberly
Kitty
Kirsten
Kirsty

L

Laura
Leanne
Lesley
Linda
Lindsey
Lisa
Lorna
Lorraine
Louisa
Louise
Lucy
Lyndsey
Lynn(e)

M

Madeleine
Mandy
Margaret
Maria
Marie
Martina
Mary
Matilda
Maureen
Maxine
Melanie
Melinda
Melissa
Merle
Michelle
Miranda

N

Nadia
Nadine
Nancy
Naomi
Natalie
Natasha
Nichola
Nicola
Nicole
Nina

O

Olivia

P

Pamela
Patricia
Paula
Pauline
Penelope
Penny
Philippa
Polly

R

Rachael
Rachel
Rebecca
Rebekah
Rita
Rosalie
Rosalind
Rosamund
Rose
Rosemary
Rowena
Ruth

S

Sadie
Sally
Sallyann
Samantha
Sandra
Sara(h)
Sharon
Sheila
Shelley
Shirley
Shona
Sonia
Sophie
Stacey
Stella
Stephanie
Susan
Susannah
Susanne
Suzanne
Sybil
Sylvia

T

Tamara
Tammy
Tamsin
Tania
Tanya
Tara
Teresa
Theresa
Tina
Tracey
Tracy

U

Ursula

V

Valerie
Vanessa
Vicki
Vicky
Victoria
Virginia
Vivien
Vivienne

W

Wendy

Y

Yolande
Yvonne

Z

Zara
Zelda
Zoe

Numbers

	Cardinal		Ordinal				Roman
1	one	s	first	ly, s	1st		I
2	two	s	second	ly, s	2nd		II
3	three	s	third	ly, .s	3rd		III
4	four	s	fourth	ly, s	4th		IV
5	five	s	fifth	ly, s	5th		V
6	six	es	sixth	ly, s	6th		VI
7	seven	s	seventh	ly, s	7th		VII
8	eight	s	eighth	ly, s	8th		VIII
9	nine	s	ninth	ly, s	9th		IX
10	ten	s	tenth	ly, s	10th		X
11	eleven	s	eleventh	s	11th		XI
12	twelve	s	twelfth	s	12th		XII
13	thirteen	s	thirteenth	s	13th		XIII
14	fourteen	s	fourteenth	s	14th		XIV
15	fifteen	s	fifteenth	s	15th		XV
16	sixteen	s	sixteenth	s	16th		XVI
17	seventeen	s	seventeenth	s	17th		XVII
18	eighteen	s	eighteenth	s	18th		XVIII
19	nineteen	s	nineteenth	s	19th		XIX
20	twent y	ies	twentieth	s	20th		XX
21	twenty-one	s	twenty-first	s	21st		XXI
22	twenty-two	s	twenty-second	s	22nd		XXII
23	twenty-three	s	twenty-third	s	23rd		XXIII
24	twenty-four	s	twenty-fourth	s	24th		XXIV
25	twenty-five	s	twenty-fifth	s	25th		XXV
26	twenty-six	es	twenty-sixth	s	26th		XXVI
27	twenty-seven	s	twenty-seventh	s	27th		XXVII
28	twenty-eight	s	twenty-eighth	s	28th		XXVIII
29	twenty-nine	s	twenty-ninth	s	29th		XXIX
30	thirt y	ies	thirtieth	s	30th		XXX
31	thirty-one	s	thirty-first	s	31st		XXXI
40	fort y	ies	fortieth	s	40th		XL
41	forty-one	s	forty-first	s	41st		XLI

	Cardinal		Ordinal		Roman	
50	fift *y*	*ies*	fiftieth	*s*	50th	L
51	fifty-one	*s*	fifty-first	*s*	51st	LI
60	sixt *y*	*ies*	sixtieth	*s*	60th	LX
61	sixty-one	*s*	sixty-first	*s*	61st	LXI
70	sevent *y*	*ies*	seventieth	*s*	70th	LXX
71	seventy-one	*s*	seventy-first	*s*	71st	LXXI
80	eight *y*	*ies*	eightieth	*s*	80th	LXXX
81	eighty-one	*s*	eighty-first	*s*	81st	LXXXI
90	ninet *y*	*ies*	ninetieth	*s*	90th	XC
91	ninety-one	*s*	ninety-first	*s*	91st	XCI
100	hundred	*s*	hundredth	*s*	100th	C
500	five hundred		five hundreth		500th	D
1,000	thousand	*s*	thousandth	*s*	1,000th	M
10,000	ten thousand		ten thousandth		10,000th	
100,000	one hundred thousand		one hundred thousandth		100,000th	
1,000,000	million	*s*	millionth	*s*	1,000,000th	

Roman numerals

When a smaller number comes *before* a larger one, it is subtracted,
e.g. IV = 5 − 1 = 4; IX = 10 − 1 = 9; XL = 50 − 10 = 40; CD = 500 − 100 = 400

When a smaller number comes *after* a larger one, it is added,
e.g. VI = 5 + 1 = 6; XI = 10 + 1 = 11; LX = 50 + 10 = 60; DC = 500 + 100 = 600

Countries and Peoples of the World

Afghanistan	Afghan	s	Ecuador	Ecuadorean	s
Albania	Albanian	s	Egypt	Egyptian	s
Algeria	Algerian	s	England	English *(plural)*	
America (see United States of America)			Ethiopia	Ethiopian	s
Angola	Angolan	s			
Argentina	Argentinian	s	Falkland Islands	Falkland Islander	s
Australia	Australian	s	Fiji	Fijian	s
Austria	Austrian	s	Finland	Finn	s
			France	French *(plural)*	
Bangladesh	Bangladeshi	s			
Belarus (see Belorussia)			Gambia	Gambian	s
Belgium	Belgian	s	Germany	German	s
Belorussia	Belorussian	s	Ghana	Ghanaian	s
Benin	Beninese		Great Britain (see Britain)		
Bhutan	Bhutanese		Greece	Greek	s
Bolivia	Bolivian	s	Guatemala	Guatemalan	s
Botswana	Citizen of Botswana		Guinea	Guinean	s
			Guyana	Guyanese	
Brazil	Brazilian	s			
Britain	British *(plural)* or Briton	s	Haiti	Haitian	s
			Holland (see Netherlands)		
Bulgaria	Bulgarian	s	Honduras	Honduran	s
Burma (now called Myanmar)	Burmese		Hong Kong	Inhabitant of Hong Kong	
			Hungary	Hungarian	s
Cambodia	Cambodian	s	Iceland	Icelander	s
Cameroon	Cameroonian	s	India	Indian	s
Canada	Canadian	s	Indonesia	Indonesian	s
Central African Republic	Person of the Central African Republic		Iran	Iranian	s
			Iraq	Iraqi	s
			Ireland, Republic of	Irish *(plural)*	
Chad	Chadian	s	Israel	Israeli	s
Chile	Chilean	s	Italy	Italian	s
China	Chinese				
Colombia	Colombian	s	Jamaica	Jamaican	s
Congo	Congolese		Japan	Japanese	
Costa Rica	Costa Rican	s	Jordan	Jordanian	s
Cuba	Cuban	s			
Cyprus	Cypriot	s	Kazakhstan	Kazakh	s
Czech Republic	Czech	s	Kenya	Kenyan	s
			Korea (North, South)	Korean	s
Denmark	Dane	s			

Kuwait	Kuwaiti	s
Lebanon	Lebanese	
Liberia	Liberian	s
Libya	Libyan	s
Luxembourg	Luxembourger	s
Madagascar	**Malagasy** *Malagasies*	
Malawi	Malawian	s
Malaysia	Malaysian	s
Mali	Malian	s
Mauritania	Mauritanian	s
Mauritius	Mauritian	s
Mexico	Mexican	s
Moldavia,		
Moldova	Moldavian	s
Monaco	Monégasque	s
Mongolia	Mongolian	s
Morocco	Moroccan	s
Mozambique	Mozambican	s
Myanmar (until 1989 called *Burma*)		
Namibia	Namibian	s
Nepal	Nepalese	
Netherlands	Dutch *(plural)*	
New Zealand	New Zealander	s
Nicaragua	Nicaraguan	s
Niger	Nigerien	s
Nigeria	Nigerian	s
Norway	Norwegian	s
Oman	Omani	s
Pakistan	Pakistani	s
Panama	Panamanian	s
Papua New Guinea	Papua New Guinean	s
Paraguay	Paraguayan	s
Peru	Peruvian	s
Philippines	Filipino	s
Poland	Pole	s
Portugal	Portuguese	
Romania	Romanian	s
Russia	Russian	s
Saudi Arabia	Saudi Arabian	s
Scotland	Scot	s
Senegal	Senegalese	

Sierra Leone	Sierra Leonean	s
Singapore	Singaporean	s
Slovakia	Slovak	s
Somalia	Somali	s
South Africa	South African	s
Spain	Spanish *(plural)*, Spaniard	s
Sri Lanka	Sri Lankan	s
Sudan	Sudanese	
Sweden	Swede	s
Switzerland	Swiss	
Syria	Syrian	s
Tanzania	Tanzanian	s
Thailand	Thai	s
Trinidad and Tobago	Trinidadian and Tobagan or Tobagonian	s
Tunisia	Tunisian	s
Turkey	Turk	s
Uganda	Ugandan	s
Ukraine	Ukrainian	s
Union of Soviet Socialist Republics (until 1991)	Russian	s
United Arab Emirates	Person of the United Arab Emirates	
United Kingdom	British *(plural)*	
United States of America	American	s
Uruguay	Uruguayan	s
Uzbekistan	Uzbek	s
Venezuela	Venezuelan	s
Vietnam	Vietnamese	
Wales	Welsh *(plural)*	
Yemen, Republic of	Yemeni	s
Zaïre	Zaïrean	s
Zambia	Zambian	s
Zimbabwe	Zimbabwean	s

Parts of Speech

Noun: A naming word, e.g. *boy, man, cat, house, Susan, England*.
On *Monday John* went by *coach* to *London Zoo* with his
teacher, *Mr. Smith*, and other *children* from his *class*.

Pronoun: A word used instead of a noun, e.g. *me, she, it, we, us, him*.
You and *I* will go now and *he* can come later with *them*.

Adjective: A word that is 'added to' a noun to describe it, e.g.
fat, thin, big, brown, green, ugly, pretty, delicious.
A *funny, little, old* man with a *large* nose and a *grey*
beard showed the *small* children his *beautiful* garden.

Verb: A doing word; a word that tells what is done, e.g.
do, go, stay, talk, shout, jump, lift, fight, eat, drink.
Stop running or you will *fall* and *hurt* yourself.

Adverb: A word that tells how, when or where something happens, e.g.
soon, often, there, now, never, quickly, carefully, carelessly.
Yesterday when I came *here* I jumped *over* that wall.

Preposition: A word that is placed before a noun, e.g.
by, in, into, at, for, under, over, against, near.
Bob went *with* his sister *on* a bus *to* the town.

Conjunction: A word that joins sentences, phrases or words, e.g.
or, than, though, although, because, while, unless.
John *and* Mary will go *if* it is fine *but* not *if* it rains.

Interjection: A word used as an exclamation, e.g. *Ah! Alas! Hey!*
Oh! You did frighten me. *Ouch!* That hurt.

Article: One of the three words – *a, an* or *the*.
A boy rode on *an* elephant at *the* zoo.

Spelling Lists of Words to Learn

The following lists contain the words you will need to use most often in your writing and compositions. You should, therefore, learn and try to remember how to spell all these words. Choose the shortest and easiest words at the beginning of each section to learn first. It is better to learn a few words each day rather than a long list, at one time, once a week. To make it easier for you the words are usually arranged in lists according to the number of letters in the words: three, four, five letters, etc. The number at the top of a word list shows the number of letters in each word in that list. Before you start to learn a list of words first study all the words in the list and notice that some words have the same letters in exactly the same order as others in the list.

All the words on pages 118 to 123 and at the bottom of page 126 are verbs, or may be used as verbs, and are arranged in lists according to the way in which their *ed*, *ing*, *s* endings are formed. When your teacher tests you on the words you have learnt he/she will probably ask you how to spell some of these words with their *ed*, *ing*, *s* endings to see whether you have understood this, e.g.

bark	**scare**	**drop**
mark *ed*	**score** *d*	**chop** *ped*
park *ing*	**stor** *ing*	**shop** *ping*
work *s*	**stone** *s*	**stop** *s*

118

You may add *ed, ing, s* to all the following words, e.g.
camp *ed, ing, s* = **camped, camping, camps**

3		4		4		4	
act	*ed, ing, s*	book	*ed, ing, s*	back	*ed, ing, s*	camp	*ed, ing, s*
add		cook		pack		damp	
air		hook		sack		bump	
arm		look		dock		dump	
ask		cool		lock		jump	
end		pool		rock		lump	
ink		show		kick		pump	
oil		slow		lick		bomb	
own		flow		pick		comb	
toy		snow		tick		lamb	

4		4		4		4	
dust	*ed, ing, s*	call	*ed, ing, s*	bark	*ed, ing, s*	load	*ed, ing, s*
last		fell		mark		boat	
list		well		park		coat	
nest		yell		work		roar	
rest		fill		cork		soap	
test		kill		fork		help	
post		mill		milk		long	
lift		will		talk		hunt	
melt		pull		walk		want	
salt		roll		bank		word	

4		4		4		4	
form	*ed, ing, s*	gain	*ed, ing, s*	head	*ed, ing, s*	bath	*ed, ing, s*
farm		pain		heal		down	
harm		rain		heat		even	
warm		pair		seat		open	
band		fail		fear		turn	
hand		jail		near		join	
land		nail		team		iron	
sand		sail		play		part	
bang		tail		pray		mind	
gang		wait		stay		view	

5		5		5		6	
clean	*ed, ing, s*	**knock**	*ed, ing, s*	**thank**	*ed, ing, s*	**answer**	*ed, ing, s*
clear		clock		train		corner	
climb		block		tramp		flower	
cloud		shock		treat		bother	
clown		black		light		gather	
chain		crack		right		matter	
chair		track		sight		master	
chalk		brick		dream		murder	
cheer		trick		radio		number	
cheat		wreck		visit		wonder	

5		5		6		6	
enter	*ed, ing, s*	**count**	*ed, ing, s*	**appear**	*ed, ing, s*	**remind**	*ed, ing, s*
cover		cough		arrest		return	
lower		rough		attack		reward	
offer		round		happen		school	
order		pound		hollow		scream	
water		sound		follow		stream	
paper		mouth		borrow		belong	
paint		group		button		poison	
point		scout		butter		powder	
plant		shout		letter		obtain	

5		5		6		7	
laugh	*ed, ing, s*	**boast**	*ed, ing, s*	**colour**	*ed, ing, s*	**explain**	*ed, ing, s*
haunt		coast		doctor		contain	
field		roast		ground		curtain	
float		toast		garden		captain	
floor		start		awaken		holiday	
flood		stamp		fasten		journey	
bloom		storm		listen		present	
stoop		allow		pocket		pretend	
spoon		enjoy		rocket		soldier	
sport		guard		ticket		station	

5		6+		6+		7+	
crawl	*ed, ing, s*	**expect**	*ed, ing, s*	**repair**	*ed, ing, s*	**disobey**	*ed, ing, s*
creak		collect		remain		discover	
crowd		correct		remind		disappear	
crown		protect		remember		disappoint	

You may add *ing* and *s* to the following words. You may not add *ed*. The words on the right of the columns are used instead.

buy	*ing, s* :	**bought**	wear	*ing, s* :	**wore, worn**
lay	:	**laid**	ring	:	**rang, rung**
pay	:	**paid**	sing	:	**sang, sung**
say	:	**said**	spring	:	**sprang, sprung**
cost	:	**cost**	sink	:	**sank, sunk**
feed	:	**fed**	drink	:	**drank, drunk**
feel	:	**felt**	think	:	**thought**
find	:	**found**	bring	:	**brought**
hear	:	**heard**	fight	:	**fought**
hold	:	**held**	build	:	**built**
hurt	*ing, s* :	**hurt**	shoot	*ing, s* :	**shot**
keep	:	**kept**	sleep	:	**slept**
lead	:	**led**	stand	:	**stood**
lend	:	**lent**	spend	:	**spent**
send	:	**sent**	sweep	:	**swept**
sell	:	**sold**	swing	:	**swung**
tell	:	**told**	spread	:	**spread**
meet	:	**met**	break	:	**broke, *n***
mean	:	**meant**	speak	:	**spoke, *n***
read	:	**read**	steal	:	**stole, *n***
see	*n, ing, s* :	**saw**	eat	*en, ing, s* :	**ate**
blow	*n, ing, s* :	**blew**	beat	*en, ing, s* :	**beat**
draw	*n, ing, s* :	**drew**	fall	*en, ing, s* :	**fell**
grow	*n, ing, s* :	**grew**			
know	*n, ing, s* :	**knew**	catch	*ing, es* :	**caught**
throw	*n, ing, s* :	**threw**	teach	*ing, es* :	**taught**

You may add *ed, ing, es* to all the following words:

box *ed, ing, es*	fish *ed, ing, es*	kiss *ed, ing, es*	fetch *ed, ing, es*
fix	dish	miss	match
mix	push	cross	watch
	rush	pass	scratch
	wash	class	march
	wish	grass	reach
	brush	guess	bunch
	crash	press	lunch
	flash	dress	touch
	finish	address	search

All the following words end in a consonant followed by a letter **e**.
You may add *d* and *s* to all the words but the **e** must be dropped before adding *ing*, e.g.

   hope *d, ęing, s* = **hoped, hoping, hopes**

4		4		4		5	
care *d, ęing, s*		dive *d, ęing, s*		hope *d, ęing, s*		argue *d, ęing, s*	
dare		tire		rope		blame	
face		fire		note		flame	
race		wire		hole		place	
save		wipe		love		dance	
wave		fine		move		piece	
hate		line		name		force	
bake		live		side		voice	
rake		like		time		price	
wake		hike		type		prize	

ę Drop **e** before adding *ing*

continued on page 122

continued from page 121

5		5		6		6	
chase	*d, ẹing, s*	**scare**	*d, ẹing, s*	**battle**	*d, ẹing, s*	**arrive**	*d, ẹing, s*
close		**score**		**bottle**		**behave**	
cause		**store**		**settle**		**chance**	
pause		**stone**		**bubble**		**bridge**	
house		**smile**		**paddle**		**change**	
amuse		**serve**		**puzzle**		**charge**	
raise		**taste**		**bundle**		**garage**	
nurse		**waste**		**double**		**damage**	
sense		**brave**		**hurdle**		**manage**	
tease		**prove**		**single**		**voyage**	

6		7		7		8	
decide	*d, ẹing, s*	**balance**	*d, ẹing, s*	**picture**	*d, ẹing, s*	**surprise**	*d, ẹing, s*
divide		**bandage**		**promise**		**exercise**	
invite		**believe**		**provide**		**exchange**	
escape		**bicycle**		**prepare**		**celebrate**	
notice		**breathe**		**produce**		**continue**	
excuse		**deserve**		**grumble**		**decorate**	
refuse		**capture**		**stumble**		**describe**	
rescue		**explore**		**tremble**		**puncture**	
circle		**imagine**		**trouble**		**struggle**	
centre		**receive**		**whistle**		**treasure**	

All the words in the left-hand columns end in a consonant followed by a letter **e**. You may add *s* to all the words but the **e** must be dropped before adding *ing*.

You may not add *d*. The words on the right of the column are used instead.

come	*ẹing, s* :	**came**		**bite**	*ẹing, s* :	**bit, bitten**
make	:	**made**		**hide**	:	**hid, hidden**
lose	:	**lost**		**ride**	:	**rode, ridden**
leave	:	**left**		**rise**	:	**rose, risen**
slide	:	**slid**		**drive**	:	**drove, driven**
strike	:	**struck**		**write**	:	**wrote, written**
				choose	:	**chose**, *n*

give	*n, ẹing, s* :	**gave**
take	*n, ẹing, s* :	**took**
shake	*n, ẹing, s* :	**shook**
mistake	*n, ẹing, s* :	**mistook**

ẹ Drop **e** before adding *ing*

You may add *s* to all the following words. The final consonant (the last letter) must be doubled before adding *ed, ing*, e.g.

drop   *ped, ping. s* = **dropped, dropping, drops**

3		3		3		4	
bat	*ted, ting, s*	**dip**	*ped, ping, s*	**beg**	*ged. ging. s*	**drop**	*ped, ping, s*
pat		**rip**		**peg**		**chop**	
pet		**tip**		**gag**		**shop**	
net		**zip**		**wag**		**stop**	
wet		**hop**		**hug**		**swop**	
fit		**pop**		**tug**		**ship**	
rot		**top**		**gun**		**slip**	
rob		**tap**		**sun**		**skip**	
mob		**map**		**pin**		**drip**	
sob		**yap**		**jab**		**grip**	

4		4		5+		5+	
trip	*ped. ping. s*	**plan**	*ned, ning. s*	**equal**	*led, ling. s*	**admit**	*ted, ting, s*
whip		**stun**		**signal**		**permit**	
clap		**grin**		**pencil**		**commit**	
snap		**skin**		**model**		**regret**	
trap		**skid**		**cancel**		**occur**	
wrap		**chat**		**parcel**		**refer**	
step		**plot**		**shovel**		**prefer**	
stab		**knot**		**travel**		**equip**	
grab		**knit**		**tunnel**		**kidnap**	
drag		**dial**		**quarrel**		**unwrap**	

None of the following words may end in *ed*.
The words in the right hand column are used instead.

get	*ting, s* :	**got**	**dig**	*ging, s* :	**dug**
set	*ting, s* :	**set**	**run**	*ning, s* :	**ran**
sit	*ting, s* :	**sat**	**win**	*ning, s* :	**won**
hit	*ting, s* :	**hit**	**spin**	*ning, s* :	**spun**
cut	*ting, s* :	**cut**	**begin**	*ning, s* :	**began, begun**
shut	*ting. s* :	**shut**	**swim**	*ming, s* :	**swam, swum**

You may add *er, est, ly, ness* to all the following words, e.g.
bold *er, est, ly, ness* = **bolder, boldest, boldly, boldness**

4		4+		5	
bold	*er, est, ly, ness*	**fair**	*er, est, ly, ness*	**light**	*er, est, ly, ness*
cold		**dear**		**tight**	
poor		**near**		**quick**	
cool		**neat**		**quiet**	
deep		**mean**		**queer**	
dark		**weak**		**steep**	
kind		**clean**		**sharp**	
loud		**clear**		**short**	
rich		**cheap**		**smart**	
slow		**great**		**thick**	
soft		**fresh**		**rough**	
wild		**clever**		**tough**	

You may add *r, st, ly, ness* to the following words:

4		4+	
late	*r, st, ly, ness*	**rude**	*r, st, ly, ness*
nice		**wide**	
fine		**large**	
safe		**close**	
sore		**fierce**	
sure		**strange**	

You may add *ly, ness* to the following words but
the last letter must be doubled before adding *er, est*.

3		3+	
sad	*der, dest, ly, ness*	**fat**	*ter, test*
mad	*der, dest*	**flat**	*ter, test*
hot	*ter, test*	**thin**	*ner, nest*
fit	*ter, test*		

All the following words end in *y*.

The *y* must be dropped before adding *ier, iest, ily, iness*, e.g.

eas *y*   *ier, iest, ily, iness* = **easier, easiest, easily, easiness**

4 +

eas *y*   *ier, iest, ily, iness*
laz *y*
tid *y*
tin *y*
ugl *y*
dirt *y*
empt *y*
heav *y*
juic *y*
luck *y*
nois *y*
rock *y*

5

happ *y*   *ier, iest, ily, iness*
sunn *y*
funn *y*
fuss *y*
mess *y*
mudd *y*
joll *y*
sill *y*
sorr *y*
shak *y*
wear *y*
wind *y*

6

stick *y ier, iest, ily, iness*
trick *y*
shabb *y*
prett *y*
lovel *y*
lonel *y*
sleep *y*
greed *y*
cheek *y*
breez *y*
gloom *y*
storm *y*

6 +

hungr *y ier, iest, ily, iness*
cloud *y*
clums *y*
chill *y*
kindl *y*
stead *y*
untid *y*
unluck *y*
naught *y*
thirst *y*
health *y*
wealth *y*

4 +

bus *y*   *ier, iest, ily*
angr *y*   *ier, iest, ily*
earl *y*   *ier, iest, iness*
sand *y*   *ier, iest, iness*
merr *y*   *ier, iest, ily, iment*

dough	also	**Monday**	**January**
cough	always	**Tuesday**	**February**
rough	almost	**Wednesday**	**March**
tough	although	**Thursday**	**April**
enough	already	**Friday**	**May**
plough	altogether	**Saturday**	**June**
through		**Sunday**	**July**
ought	all right		**August**
bought		spring	**September**
brought		summer	**October**
fought		autumn	**November**
thought		winter	**December**

All the following words end in **y**.
You may add *ing* but the **y** must be dropped before adding *ied, ies.*

cry	*ing*	**carry**	*ing*	**copy**	*ing*
cr *ied*	*ies*	**carr** *ied*	*ies*	**cop** *ied*	*ies*
dry	*ing*	**marry**	*ing*	**bury**	*ing*
dr *ied*	*ies*	**marr** *ied*	*ies*	**bur** *ied*	*ies*
try	*ing*	**hurry**	*ing*	**tidy**	*ing*
tr *ied*	*ies*	**hurr** *ied*	*ies*	**tid** *ied*	*ies*
fry	*ing*	**worry**	*ing*	**occupy**	*ing*
fr *ied*	*ies*	**worr** *ied*	*ies*	**occup** *ied*	*ies*
spy	*ing*	**empty**	*ing*	**satisfy**	*ing*
sp *ied*	*ies*	**empt** *ied*	*ies*	**satisf** *ied*	*ies*
fly	*ing*	**study**	*ing*	**terrify**	*ing*
fl *ies*		**stud** *ied*	*ies*	**terrif** *ied*	*ies*
flew, flown					

A very few verbs end in **ie**. You may add *d* and *s* but the **ie** must be changed to *y* before adding *ing*.

die	*d, s*	**lie**	*d, s*	**tie**	*d, s*
dy *ing*		**ly** *ing*		**ty** *ing*	

Singular		Plural	Singular	Plural	Singular	Plural
foot		feet	bab *y*	*ies*	key	*s*
goose		geese	lad *y*	*ies*	donkey	*s*
tooth		teeth	bod *y*	*ies*	monkey	*s*
mouse		mice	pon *y*	*ies*	valley	*s*
man		men	cit *y*	*ies*	chimney	*s*
woman		women	arm *y*	*ies*	cowboy	*s*
child		children	nav *y*	*ies*	railway	*s*
			aunt *y*	*ies*	gangway	*s*
life		lives	dadd *y*	*ies*	holiday	*s*
wife		wives	mumm *y*	*ies*	birthday	*s*
knife		knives				
			dais *y*	*ies*	zoo	*s*
leaf		leaves	dair *y*	*ies*	piano	*s*
loaf		loaves	fair *y*	*ies*	radio	*s*
thief		thieves	stor *y*	*ies*		
			part *y*	*ies*	hero	*es*
dwarf	*s* or	dwarves	jell *y*	*ies*	cargo	*es*
scarf	*s* or	scarves	lorr *y*	*ies*	Negro	*es*
wharf	*s* or	wharves	pupp *y*	*ies*	potato	*es*
hoof	*s* or	hooves	hobb *y*	*ies*	tomato	*es*
roof	*s*		enem *y*	*ies*	volcano	*es*
elf		elves	canar *y*	*ies*	bus	*es*
calf		calves	famil *y*	*ies*	glass	*es*
half		halves	grann *y*	*ies*	beach	*es*
wolf		wolves	cherr *y*	*ies*	peach	*es*
shelf		shelves	countr *y*	*ies*	torch	*es*
			librar *y*	*ies*	witch	*es*
self		selves	factor *y*	*ies*	church	*es*
itself			robber *y*	*ies*	circus	*es*
myself			myster *y*	*ies*	princess	*es*
himself			discover *y*	*ies*	sandwich	*es*
herself						
yourself		yourselves	**every**	*body, one, thing, where*		
		ourselves	**any**	*body, one, thing, where, how, way*		
		themselves	**some**	*body, one, thing, where, how, times*		

4	4	5	4		4		5	
able	than	these	bell	s	bird	s	giant	s
away	that	those	ball	s	desk	s	glove	s
best	then	where	wall	s	lake	s	green	s
born	them	which	hall	s	lawn	s	hedge	s
both	they	while	hill	s	lion	s	horse	s
does	this	whole	cake	s	neck	s	hotel	s
done	true	whose	card	s	nose	s	jewel	s
goes	luck	worse	cart	s	page	s	lemon	s
gone	ever	worst	cave	s	path	s	noise	s
gold	very	worth	case	s	pond	s	ocean	s

4	4	5	4		4		5	
dead	went	could	coal	s	shed	s	other	s
deaf	were	would	goal	s	shoe	s	owner	s
each	what	magic	door	s	sock	s	plate	s
else	when	might	food	s	song	s	fruit	s
just	with	money	moon	s	tent	s	pupil	s
must	clay	music	room	s	town	s	purse	s
much	beef	never	wood	s	tree	s	queen	s
many	pork	pence	wool	s	mile	s	salad	s
more	east	sugar	flag	s	your	s	shirt	s
most	west	ready	frog	s	year	s	snake	s

4	5	5	4		5		5	
from	about	among	game	s	apple	s	stair	s
next	above	below	gate	s	baker	s	stick	s
none	after	blood	gift	s	bread	s	stove	s
only	again	earth	hole	s	beast	s	sword	s
once	ahead	often	home	s	cabin	s	table	s
upon	alone	sorry	hour	s	cloth	s	thing	s
same	along	sheep	king	s	comic	s	tiger	s
some	alike	shall	kite	s	dozen	s	truck	s
soon	alive	under	knee	s	front	s	white	s
such	aside	until	idea	s	ghost	s	world	s

6	7	6		6		9	
across	against	friend	s	infant	s	adventure	s
afraid	another	forest	s	insect	s	aeroplane	s
around	because	finger	s	inside	s	afternoon	s
asleep	beneath	father	s	island	s	chocolate	s
ashore	between	mother	s	desert	s	favourite	s
awhile	clothes	leader	s	orange	s	passenger	s
before	instead	reader	s	second	s	newspaper	s
behind	nothing	saucer	s	minute	s	orchestra	s
better	perhaps	sister	s	moment	s	programme	s
cattle	without	reason	s	museum	s	vegetable	s

6	8	6		7			
during	together	bullet	s	bedroom	s	full	y
either	tomorrow	carrot	s	blanket	s	awful	ly
famous	horrible	coffee	s	brother	s	useful	ly
hardly	horribly	cotton	s	teacher	s	careful	ly
little	terrible	dinner	s	sausage	s	playful	ly
middle	terribly	kitten	s	cabbage	s	cheerful	ly
modern	possible	lesson	s	cottage	s	dreadful	ly
unless	possibly	rabbit	s	message	s	thankful	ly
utmost	probable	robber	s	village	s	beautiful	ly
within	probably	rubber	s	lettuce	s	forgetful	ly
						wonderful	ly

6	6		6		7			
people	animal	s	parent	s	chicken	s	helpful	ly
petrol	banana	s	person	s	kitchen	s	hopeful	ly
plenty	beside	s	prince	s	husband	s	skilful	ly
police	bucket	s	secret	s	pudding	s	faithful	ly
rather	castle	s	street	s	morning	s	grateful	ly
really	cousin	s	string	s	evening	s	peaceful	ly
safety	coward	s	violin	s	tadpole	s	powerful	ly
should	danger	s	window	s	tractor	s	spiteful	ly
seldom	engine	s	pillow	s	visitor	s	delightful	ly
silver	needle	s	yellow	s	outside	s	disgraceful	ly

Contractions *(shortened words)*

These are words which have been shortened by joining two words together and placing an apostrophe where a letter or letters have been left out. Learn the words and the contractions, being very careful to remember exactly where the apostrophe goes.

can't = cannot
don't = do not
won't = will not
isn't = is not
aren't = are not
didn't = did not
hadn't = had not
hasn't = has not
wasn't = was not
shan't = shall not
doesn't = does not
haven't = have not
mustn't = must not
needn't = need not
weren't = were not
couldn't = could not
wouldn't = would not
shouldn't = should not

he's = he is;   he has
she's = she is;   she has
it's = it is
who's = who is
that's = that is
what's = what is
here's = here is
there's = there is

I'll = I will;   I shall
we'll = we will;   we shall
he'll = he will;   he shall
she'll = she will;   she shall
you'll = you will;   you shall
who'll = who will;   who shall
they'll = they will;   they shall

I'd = I had;   I would
he'd = he had;   he would
we'd = we had;   we would
you'd = you had;   you would
who'd = who had;   who would
they'd = they had;   they would

we're = we are
you're = you are
who're = who are
they're = they are

I've = I have
we've = we have
you've = you have
they've = they have

I'm = I am

The apostrophe is also used to show possession, e.g.

The boy's book;   girl's coat;   man's car;   woman's watch.
The boys' books;   girls' coats;   men's cars;   women's watches.

Homophones

These are words that sound alike but have different meanings and spellings.

arc	(curve)	pain	(suffering)	accept	(receive)
ark	(boat; box)	pane	(of glass)	except	(leaving out)
beach	(seashore)	pair	(two)	allowed	(let; permitted)
beech	(tree)	pear	(fruit)	aloud	(loudly)
bean	(plant)	peace	(quiet)	altar	(church table)
been	(past of be)	piece	(a part)	alter	(change)
blew	(blow)	peer	(stare)	dear	(beloved; costly)
blue	(colour)	pier	(jetty)	deer	(animal)
bough	(branch)	place	(position)	flour	(ground wheat)
bow	(bend)	plaice	(fish)	flower	(blossom)
brake	(to stop)	rap	(knock)	foul	(dirty; unfair)
break	(to snap)	wrap	(cover)	fowl	(bird)
chute	(a slide)	sail	(ship)	freeze	(ice; cold)
shoot	(fire)	sale	(selling)	frieze	(wall decoration)
die	(lose life)	slay	(kill)	groan	(moan)
dye	(colour)	sleigh	(sled)	grown	(got bigger)
farther	(further)	stair	(step)	guessed	(did guess)
father	(parent)	stare	(look at)	guest	(visitor)
fort	(castle)	steal	(thieve)	hear	(listen)
fought	(fight)	steel	(metal)	here	(in this place)
hair	(of head)	tail	(end)	heard	(listened)
hare	(animal)	tale	(story)	herd	(of cattle, etc.)
hart	(stag)	pail	(bucket)	hoard	(hidden store)
heart	(of body)	pale	(whitish)	horde	(crowd)
heal	(cure)	scene	(view; place)	hour	(sixty minutes)
heel	(of foot)	seen	(noticed)	our	(belonging to us)
higher	(taller)	tire	(weary)	hole	(hollow place)
hire	(rent)	tyre	(wheel cover)	whole	(all; complete)
hoarse	(husky)	weak	(not strong)	meat	(flesh)
horse	(animal)	week	(seven days)	meet	(come together)
leant	(leaned)	weather	(climate)	meter	(measuring box)
lent	(lend)	whether	(if)	metre	(length measure)
made	(make)	wood	(timber)	moan	(groan)
maid	(girl)	would	(past of will)	mown	(cut grass, etc.)
muscle	(of body)	won	(did win)	signet	(seal, ring)
mussel	(shellfish)	one	(single)	cygnet	(young swan)

knew	(know)	**shore**	(seashore)
new	(just made)	**sure**	(certain)
knight	(Sir)	**their**	(belonging to them)
night	(opp. of day)	**there**	(in that place)
know	(understand)	**they're**	(they are)
no	(not any; opp. of yes)	**theirs**	(belonging to them)
knot	(tied string, etc.)	**there's**	(there is)
not	(no)	**threw**	(throw)
passed	(did pass)	**through**	(from end to end)
past	(time gone by)	**throne**	(king's seat)
ring	(circle; bell sound)	**thrown**	(throw)
wring	(twist)	**board**	(wood; go on ship; lodge)
wait	(stay; serve)	**bored**	(weary; drilled hole)
weight	(Heaviness)	**cereal**	(wheat, oats, etc.)
way	(direction)	**serial**	(in parts)
weigh	(measure heaviness)	**currant**	(fruit)
waste	(not used; useless)	**current**	(flow of water, air, etc.)
waist	(of body)	**cue**	(hint; billiard-stick)
which	(what one? who?)	**queue**	(line of persons, etc.)
witch	(old woman)	**fair**	(just; light; entertainment)
who's	(who is)	**fare**	(price of journey; food)
whose	(belonging to whom?)	**core**	(middle of apple, etc.)
you're	(you are)	**corps**	(group of cadets, etc.)
your	(belonging to you)	**road**	(highway)
it's	(it is)	**rode**	(ride)
its	(belonging to it)	**rowed**	(used oars)
pedal	(foot lever)	**cent**	(coin)
peddle	(to hawk goods)	**sent**	(send)
hall	(room; passage)	**scent**	(smell; perfume)
haul	(pull; amount taken)	**rain**	(water)
him	(he)	**reign**	(rule)
hymn	(song of praise)	**rein**	(strap)
mare	(female horse)	**buy**	(purchase)
mayor	(head of town or city)	**by**	(near to, etc.)
medal	(badge – for bravery, etc.)	**bye**	(a run)
meddle	(interfere)	**to**	(towards)
pray	(ask God)	**too**	(also; more than enough)
prey	(victim; thing hunted)	**two**	(number)

Multiplication Tables

0 × 2 = 0	0 × 3 = 0	0 × 4 = 0	0 × 5 = 0
1 × 2 = 2	1 × 3 = 3	1 × 4 = 4	1 × 5 = 5
2 × 2 = 4	2 × 3 = 6	2 × 4 = 8	2 × 5 = 10
3 × 2 = 6	3 × 3 = 9	3 × 4 = 12	3 × 5 = 15
4 × 2 = 8	4 × 3 = 12	4 × 4 = 16	4 × 5 = 20
5 × 2 = 10	5 × 3 = 15	5 × 4 = 20	5 × 5 = 25
6 × 2 = 12	6 × 3 = 18	6 × 4 = 24	6 × 5 = 30
7 × 2 = 14	7 × 3 = 21	7 × 4 = 28	7 × 5 = 35
8 × 2 = 16	8 × 3 = 24	8 × 4 = 32	8 × 5 = 40
9 × 2 = 18	9 × 3 = 27	9 × 4 = 36	9 × 5 = 45
10 × 2 = 20	10 × 3 = 30	10 × 4 = 40	10 × 5 = 50
11 × 2 = 22	11 × 3 = 33	11 × 4 = 44	11 × 5 = 55
12 × 2 = 24	12 × 3 = 36	12 × 4 = 48	12 × 5 = 60

0 × 6 = 0	0 × 7 = 0	0 × 8 = 0	0 × 9 = 0
1 × 6 = 6	1 × 7 = 7	1 × 8 = 8	1 × 9 = 9
2 × 6 = 12	2 × 7 = 14	2 × 8 = 16	2 × 9 = 18
3 × 6 = 18	3 × 7 = 21	3 × 8 = 24	3 × 9 = 27
4 × 6 = 24	4 × 7 = 28	4 × 8 = 32	4 × 9 = 36
5 × 6 = 30	5 × 7 = 35	5 × 8 = 40	5 × 9 = 45
6 × 6 = 36	6 × 7 = 42	6 × 8 = 48	6 × 9 = 54
7 × 6 = 42	7 × 7 = 49	7 × 8 = 56	7 × 9 = 63
8 × 6 = 48	8 × 7 = 56	8 × 8 = 64	8 × 9 = 72
9 × 6 = 54	9 × 7 = 63	9 × 8 = 72	9 × 9 = 81
10 × 6 = 60	10 × 7 = 70	10 × 8 = 80	10 × 9 = 90
11 × 6 = 66	11 × 7 = 77	11 × 8 = 88	11 × 9 = 99
12 × 6 = 72	12 × 7 = 84	12 × 8 = 96	12 × 9 = 108

0 × 10 = 0	0 × 11 = 0	0 × 12 = 0
1 × 10 = 10	1 × 11 = 11	1 × 12 = 12
2 × 10 = 20	2 × 11 = 22	2 × 12 = 24
3 = 10 = 30	3 × 11 = 33	3 × 12 = 36
4 × 10 = 40	4 × 11 = 44	4 × 12 = 48
5 × 10 = 50	5 × 11 = 55	5 × 12 = 60
6 × 10 = 60	6 × 11 = 66	6 × 12 = 72
7 × 10 = 70	7 × 11 = 77	7 × 12 = 84
8 × 10 = 80	8 × 11 = 88	8 × 12 = 96
9 × 10 = 90	9 × 11 = 99	9 × 12 = 108
10 × 10 = 100	10 × 11 = 110	10 × 12 = 120
11 × 10 = 110	11 × 11 = 121	11 × 12 = 132
12 × 10 = 120	12 × 11 = 132	12 × 12 = 144

Note for Teachers and Parents

Spell It Yourself is based on the belief that there is need for a new type of book which is neither a dictionary nor a conventional spelling book.

Most school children are encouraged to refer to dictionaries for words they wish to use in their written work. But school dictionaries have been compiled, in the first place, for the giving of definitions: the choice of words is usually dictated by children's problems of understanding rather than of spelling. As a result, many everyday words which nevertheless present spelling difficulties are not in school dictionaries, because children are sure to know their meaning.

Some of the commonest spelling errors are made in forming derivatives from root-words which in themselves are quite easy to spell. For example, a child probably knows—or could easily find from a dictionary—how to spell these infinitives: differ, prefer, happen, begin, come, singe, sail, dial, shop, gallop, argue, agree, queue, picnic,, deny, tie, forget, fidget. But there will probably be nothing in the dictionary to help the child to the correct spelling of their present and past participles. How is he or she to know, for example, that the correct forms are 'shopping, shopped', and not 'shoping, shoped'? If the child remembers the doubling of that final consonant, how is he or she to know that the mistake of 'picnicing, picniced' must be corrected by writing 'picnicking, picnicked', and not 'picniccing, picnicced'? Other difficult and irregular word-derivatives not usually in dictionaries include plurals and the comparatives and superlatives of adjectives.

Certain spelling rules may be worked out, but most of these are confused by their many exceptions, and so are of limited usefulness, especially with younger children.

Clearly, children are likely to learn to spell correctly words which they are anxious to use in their own writing. In free writing, children are often not content to mis-spell, if they can avoid it; and they may waste much time, at the expense of the content of their written work, trying to discover the correct spelling of words they need. The usual school spelling-books of groups of words for memorization, children's own word-books, and most junior dictionaries cannot give proper guidance. The teacher often has little time to help with individual problems. It is hoped that this book, *Spell It Yourself*, will provide a useful tool, easy for children to handle for themselves as they need.

Spelling—with the exception of a limited number of the commonest words—seems a subject for individual learning: no two children wish to make use of exactly the same words in their written expression. This reference list, of nearly 8,000 root words, is based upon word-frequency in the upper classes of Junior and Middle Schools; but the list also includes many of the less common words which individual children may need.

In their written compositions children use words whose meanings they understand. They do not often need definitions of the words they cannot spell. Children's ability to read and recognize words is much greater than their ability to spell them; in this book they should be able quickly to find and identify the words they hesitate to spell. The order of the words is alphabetical, and if a child knows the first two letters—as he or she usually does—of the word required, the child can find in the Index the number of the page where he or she should look for it.

The alphabetical basis of the book provides useful training in the use of a dictionary. At the same time, *Spell It Yourself* makes a point of including many words which a school dictionary does not. Word-derivatives are usually shown by suffixes to the right of the columns which need only to be added to the root-words (see the Instructions).

In general, children learn best by finding out for themselves. In this book they will learn to look up words for themselves and to spell them correctly the first time, instead of making mistakes which have later to be corrected. They will steadily increase their written vocabulary, becoming more 'word-conscious' all the time. With this book at their elbow, and under the direction of a teacher aware of its purpose, they will be teaching themselves how to spell.

Index

A
		Page
ab, ac		1
ad, ae, af, ag		2
ai, al, am		3
an, ap		4
aq, ar, as		5
at, au, av		6
aw, ax		7

B
ba		7
be		8
bi		9
bl, bo		10
br		11
bu		12
by		13

C
ca		13
ce, ch		15
ci, cl		17
co		18
cr		21
cu		22
cy		23

D
da		23
de		24
di		25
do, dr		27
du, dw, dy		28

E
ea, ec, ed, ee		29
ef, eg, ei, el		29
em, en		30
ep, eq, er		31
es, ev		31
ex		32
ey		33

F
		Page
fa, fe		33
fi		34
fl		35
fo		36
fr, fu		37

G
ga		38
ge, gh, gi, gl		39
gn, go, gr		40
gu, gy		42

H
ha		42
he		43
hi, ho		44
hu		45
hy		46

I
ic, id, ig, il		46
im, in		47
ir, is, it, iv		49

J
ja		49
je, ji		50
jo, ju		50

K
ka		51
ke, kh		51
ki, kn		51

L
la		52
le, li		53
lo		54
lu, ly		55

M
ma		55
me		57
mi		58
mo		59
mu, my		60

		Page
N	na	61
	ne, ni	61
	no, nu, ny	62
O	oa	62
	ob, oc, od, of	63
	og, oi, ol	63
	om, on, op	64
	or, os, ot	64
	ou, ov	65
	ow, ox, oy	65
P	pa	66
	pe	67
	ph, pi	68
	pl, po	69
	pr	71
	pu	72
	py	73
Q	qua	73
	que	73
	qui, quo	73
R	ra, re	74
	rh, ri, ro	77
	ru	78
S	sa	78
	sc	79
	se	80
	sh	81
	si	83
	sk, sl	84
	sm, sn	85
	so, sp	86
	sq, st	88
	su	90
	sw	91
	sy	92

		Page
T	ta	92
	te	93
	th	94
	ti, to	95
	tr	96
	tu, tw, ty	98
U	ug, um	98
	un	99
	up, ur, us	100
	ut	101
V	va, ve	101
	vi	102
	vo, vu	102
W	wa	102
	we	103
	wh	104
	wi, wo	105
	wr	106
X	x-r	106
	xy	106
Y	ya	106
	ye	106
	yi, yo	107
Z	ze, zi, zo, zu	107
Boys' Names		108
Girls' Names		110
Numbers		112
Countries and Peoples of the World		114
Parts of Speech		116
Lists of Words to Learn		117
Contractions		130
Homophones		131
Multiplication Tables		133
Note for Teachers and Parents		134